Make your money work for you

ANTHEA GARDNER

MAKE YOUR MONEY WORK FOR YOU

Think big, start small

Jonathan Ball Publishers
Johannesburg & Cape Town

Published in South Africa in 2019 by
JONATHAN BALL PUBLISHERS
A division of Media24 (Pty) Ltd
PO Box 33977
Jeppestown
2043

ISBN 978-1-86842-970-7
ebook ISBN 978-1-86842-971-4

*Every effort has been made to trace the copyright holders and to
obtain their permission for the use of copyright material.
The publishers apologise for any errors or omissions and would be grateful
to be notified of any corrections that should be incorporated
in future editions of this book.*

Twitter: www.twitter.com/JonathanBallPub
Facebook: www.facebook.com/JonathanBallPublishers
Blog: http://jonathanball.bookslive.co.za/

Cover by publicide
Design and typesetting by Nazli Jacobs
Set in 10,5 on 16pt Veljovic

This book is dedicated to every person who has ever worried about saving, investing or retirement. Read this book with a pencil in your hand and feel free to make notes in the margins.

Contents

Introduction

Five years ago I started an asset management business and called it Cartesian Capital, after the French philosopher and mathematician René Descartes. He is best known for the saying, 'I think therefore I am', and his mathematical legacy includes the x-axis and y-axis plane. The string of numbers your GPS uses are called 'Cartesian coordinates', after Descartes.

Before that, I earned my stripes on trading floors and investment teams for large international banks, where I traded and invested such large sums of money that it often felt a bit surreal. But I've learned that every investment decision I take is important to the ordinary investor – you.

This book will show you how to take control of your financial future and how to make your hard-earned cash work harder for you – what we sometimes refer to as 'sweating your assets'. For the record, your assets include your house, investments and cash.

Whether you're a salaried employee with a company pension fund, a brave entrepreneur with overheads to meet every month or a future entrepreneur, this book will introduce you to the exciting world of investing and give you the knowledge you need to create wealth with your salary or savings. The goal is to retire comfortably, gain financial independence, create your personal discretionary spending fund, or all of the above.

Ideally, it is best to start investing as soon as you start earning a salary, but I understand that not everyone was given that advice or shown how to do it when they started working. I advocate starting as soon as possible to take advantage of a system that is set up to help you grow the money you earn. Even if you're in your fifties – start now.

Whether you've got R500 000, R50 000, R5 000 or R500 there is no excuse not to start investing as soon as possible. No matter how small or large the amount, with a 12% per annum return you will double your money every six years. Look out for the Rule of 72 in Chapter 8; you won't believe how easy it is to do the calculation and impress your friends.

This book will also introduce you to the concept of risk-taking and how to apply it to your personal circumstances. I'll teach you the difference between an exchange-traded fund (ETF), a managed fund and a unit trust; why you need a retirement annuity (RA) as well as a pension fund; and how to be tax-efficient with your investments.

If one day you decide, like Jeff Bezos, that you want to give up the regularity of a monthly salary and those eye-watering bonuses, commissions or thirteenth cheques to start your own business from your garage, this book will help you create a safety net, put food on the table, and pay the mortgage while you establish your brand and build a financially successful business.

Of course, not everyone dreams of starting the next Amazon, and you might be content that your corporate job affords you a monthly income, sometimes accompanied by a subsidised pension fund and medical aid. However, maybe your son will turn out to be a tennis prodigy who needs to travel to Los Angeles, where all the top tennis coaches are based, or maybe your daughter will be the one who needs you to help cover her rent while she creates the next Facebook from her room in university residence.

So why not create the financial stability that will allow you to give them that helping hand? And if it turns out that they don't need it, well, there's nothing wrong with having money to travel the world in your retirement, paying for life-saving surgery, or not having to worry about whether you will have enough money to live to 100.

I want to demystify investments and the stock market and show you how to invest wisely. While I will do my best to avoid all the technical concepts and jargon, a few basics must be covered. It's important to know the difference between saving and investing, what your personal risk profile looks like, and how to invest to achieve *your* personal financial goals (we're not so worried about anyone else right now, but if you are, then pass this book on to them when you're done).

When a financial advisor is told not to use jargon, or when their client tells them they know nothing about investments, the advisor's immediate reaction is to 'dumb it down' and talk down to the person in front of them. This book does not do that. I'm going to assume that you are smart and thoughtful enough to understand your personal financial situation (because that's what this is all about), and I'm going to assume you want to take the time to think about the concepts and ideas I present in the chapters that follow.

I'm sure you know how to use Google to find more information. If you still have questions, email me at invest@cartesian.co.za or visit www.thinkbigstartsmall.co.za.

1

Why not simply spend it all?

If you don't know where you are going,
any road can take you there.
– Lewis Carroll, *Alice's Adventures in Wonderland*

As an asset manager, I interact directly with clients, who include my sister and my brother-in-law. In the last couple of years, I have realised that our industry uses a lot of jargon, and not just any kind of jargon, but scary jargon.

Even my sister, who is clever and worldly-wise and who grew up with both parents working in banking and finance, had very little idea of the simplest concepts that I take for granted. After several conversations with her and my brother-in-law about how they could invest, I realised that even though they were smart enough to know they needed to invest, they were too anxious to go to a financial planner. Not only because they thought they needed millions to engage with an investment manager, but also because it's daunting when you don't even know what questions to ask, or what to look out for.

Furthermore, they'd just had their second child. Children cost money, so why even bother to save or invest when the children need so much? At least, that was their thinking.

They are not alone. I find that many people are intimidated by the concept of investing. They believe it's a complex and abstract thing that can be done only by professionals.

I have news for you. If you have a home, a car or a career, you already have investments. You've put time and hard-earned money into these assets. If you already have one or more of these investments, the only real question is whether it's a good investment.

Think about it: if investing is about making money, then surely your career is an investment. I'm not here to give you career advice, but I would recommend you treat your work hours with an expectation that you will generate a return. Define your career goals. Plan your career. Be fastidious about getting the best return on your hours invested.

It is much easier than you might think to invest in the stock market. If you set and achieve basic personal financial goals, you'll be able to achieve financial independence simply by using your salary.

Many people confuse financial independence with financial freedom. Financial freedom is a generic term used to explain the feeling individuals get when they are in a position to purchase whatever they need and don't have to panic when unexpected expenses crop up. For some people, it's about being able to put food on the table; for others, it's about being able to afford a fancy car, to send their children to private school, or not to worry about the exchange rate while on an overseas holiday. For some, financial freedom is as simple as earning a decent salary every month.

My question to that person is, what happens if the company you work for closes down? We should then strive for financial *independence*, which means we have enough wealth and reserves to live without being dependent on a salary.

One of the most common misconceptions about investing is that you must be rich to invest. While investing R5 a month won't make you the next Bill Gates, you do need to start somewhere, and the sooner you start, the easier it will be down the line. Some funds require no minimum investment and other platforms offer investments for as little as R100.

Consumers in emerging markets like ours hold a particular fascination for me. Consumerism seems to be the curse of most South Africans. I understand that suddenly having access to wealth makes it tempting to go out and buy all the nice things you could never afford before, but I also think that spending or saving money is a cultural phenomenon.

Why is it that China and India have high savings rates, while South Africa has a horrendously low savings rate? Chinese and Indian households save 40% and 30% of their income, respectively, while South African households put aside less than 5%.

Why bother saving, investing and growing your financial safety net? Many people ask, why can't they just live and enjoy life in the here and now? The future will take care of itself, won't it?

Let me tell you, it won't.

Let me share a story or two from my experiences in taking part in Ironman triathlon competitions. I enjoy triathlons, to the point where I even had a coach for a couple of years. I used to get a weekly email from Donovan, my cyber-coach, which I'd read to check my daily programme. Almost every day I would read the tagline: 'Today I do what others won't, so tomorrow I can accomplish what others cannot.'[1]

This powerful message saw me through a couple of sprint-distance[2] triathlons in Cape Town, Johannesburg and London, and a few Olympic-distance triathlons, including the world's largest – the London and the Paris triathlons. It also encouraged me to triple my training so that I could do a half Ironman on the beautiful island of Mallorca and some other scenic locations around the world. And when I decided (actually, I think I might have been pushed by my coach and coerced by my training partners in Tunis, where I worked at the time) to do the full Ironman in Sweden, it was those words that got me out of bed at 4 am through summer and winter, onto my bike, into my trainers and, worse still, into a cold-water swimming pool at ungodly hours, to achieve my goal.

The sacrifices were hard to stomach, and the discipline required was almost superhuman. But today I can say that on a cold morning in September 2012, I got up before the sun, force-fed myself a high-energy breakfast, put on my tri-suit, checked and racked my bike in the transition area, packed my cycling and running gear, squeezed into my wetsuit and walked down to the pier in Kalmar, a beautiful town on the Baltic Sea.

When the starting gun went off, I ignored the butterflies and started a 15-hour journey of swimming in the cold Baltic, cycling on the island of Öland (in the rain), and running the streets and forests of Kalmar. All the while I was talking to myself, thinking why, oh why, have I willingly brought such pain on myself?

But when I crossed the finish line and I heard legendary Ironman announcer Paul Kaye say, 'Anthea. You. Are. An. Ironman', I knew exactly why.

More than pride, I felt a huge sense of accomplishment.

The thing is, doing an Ironman is a bit like investing. It's a long-term goal that requires quite a bit of sacrifice, but it is incredibly satisfying crossing the finishing line and knowing it was you, and only you, who did it. At the end of an Ironman, there is a sense of accomplishment worth infinitely more than instant gratification.

An Ironman consists of a 3,8-km swim, 180-km cycle and 42,2-km run (all of that before the 17-hour midnight cut-off). It's big and audacious by anyone's standards. But there is simplicity in achieving the goal. Have a plan, stick to the plan, and just put one foot in front of the other.

Equally, you will only succeed financially if you know why you're doing it. If you want financial independence badly enough, you will set the time aside to plan for it and you will make the necessary sacrifices. Whatever your personal reason, get your mind right – make the decision to think big even if you have to start small.

Every single person has their own reason for taking control of their money. One person might have ambitions to leave her boring corporate job to start her own small business; another might want the freedom to travel, to have money to see her through a possible redundancy or simply to ensure there's a roof over her family's head. The list is endless.

I've found my personal good reason for taking control of my money. It has been proven that financial stress lowers your IQ by a full 13 points. That's right! Stress lowers glucose levels and negatively impacts the frontal cortex of the brain, which is responsible for attention and discipline. According to an article in the journal *Science*, people who worried about money experienced, on average, a 13-point drop in their IQ, which is the same impact as sleep-deprivation torture.[3]

Being poor is stressful. Financial stability, on the other hand, affords you the freedom to grow, not only materially, but also intellectually.

Everyone thinks long and hard about choosing a career, or buying a home and a car, but as they get closer to their sixties, suddenly they start panicking about whether or not they will have enough money to retire. We need to think about saving and investing as a rite of passage to being a grown-up. It must become second nature.

Let me show you how to take control – right now!

Before we set out on our journey to set personal financial goals and achieve financial independence, we need to investigate our attitude towards money.

Money is *not* a dirty word. I know many people were taught not to speak about money; it was considered tactless. I can't specifically remember my parents telling me that it was impolite to speak about money, but for many years somewhere deep inside me was the feeling that it was not the right thing to do. But today I firmly believe this is an outmoded way to think about money.

I meet quite a few wealthy people in my line of work, and I have learned to distinguish between those who know that their worth is based on the type of person they are, and those who pursue reckless, unnecessary consumerism and believe their worth is based on displaying their wealth. The first group may have the latest designer gear and drive expensive cars, but they stand in direct opposition to the shallow person who will do anything for money. What makes the first group different (and no, it's not about old money versus new money) is their attitude to money, the people around them and the world. As much as disrespecting money is bad, so is worshipping it. But money in itself is not bad.

So, what is your attitude to money? Do you think like a wealthy person? Or do you despise capitalism? Do you see money as a means to an end? Or do you realise that large amounts of money come with freedom and the power to do good in the world? I bet some of you even baulked when you read the phrase 'large amounts of money'. You need to get over it. How can you attract money if you are disgusted by it?

If you think money is evil, I have a challenge for you: go out and make enough of it so that you buy yourself a decent home, security for your family and fabulous holidays. Or, better yet, use that money to go out and build a school in a village in rural Africa, fill it with books, and pay the teachers enough to support their own families. And then let's have an informed debate about the evils of money.

Recently, it has become quite fashionable to believe that the world needs another way of transacting, especially with the advent of cryptocurrencies, such as Bitcoin. I do want to remind everyone that cryptocurrency started out as a way for bad people to transact in a manner that would ensure they wouldn't be caught. Somehow it became touted as the next best investment.

The first step to becoming wealthy is when you start to think like a wealthy person. Wealthy people do not become wealthy by disregarding money or taking it for granted. There's no need to make money the centre of your universe, but you do need to take the time to understand what you want and how you're going to get it.

I'm lucky in that my job is centred around making money for other people, and so it's my 'main gig', but I can understand that it might not be your main focus. Luckily for you, there are a number of people like me in the world who will handle the everyday routine of making investment decisions. Some of those people are pretty darn good at it too.

Your job, and why you're reading this book, is to understand your personal goals. This will give you a better idea which of those investment professionals to trust, which to question, and how to instruct them to deliver the best outcome for you.

KEY POINTS

■ Money is not the root of all evil. You deserve to be wealthy! And having money gives you the ability to affect the world positively.

■ Making money is not complicated. Let's get on and do it!

2

Setting your financial goals

We all know the saying, 'A penny saved is a penny earned', famously attributed to Benjamin Franklin. The Franklin Society, an online investment information service, would say this is a misquotation and the correct version is, 'A penny saved is two-pence dear',[4] but this is much of a muchness really.

The message is clear: stop excessive spending. This is the only way to grow your wealth.

In its most basic form, saving is buying the two-for-one shampoo special. It's drinking tap water instead of bottled water, foregoing that expensive takeaway lunch for last night's leftovers, and taking all those coins and squirrelling them away.

If I do save a penny, how does it become two? Let me extrapolate: in a year's time a penny saved is worth a penny less the rate of inflation. If you had R100 in cash right now, you could buy something worth R100 today or you could put it in a porcelain piggy bank and take it out after one year. If the inflation rate was 5%, by the time you took out that R100, in essence, you could only buy 95,2% of the same item from a year ago because the R100 item will now cost

R105 (R100/R105 = 95.2%). If you'd spent it on day one, whatever you bought with your R100 is likely to have depreciated in value and would still be worth less than the R100 you spent on it a year ago.

However, if you were clever and bought an asset that appreciates in value by at least the rate of inflation, then it would be worth the same or more. Isn't this what we would all like to do? In this book I want to show you how you can use your salary to save a penny and turn it into two, or three, or four!

When you're saving (squirrelling away), you want stability of capital. You want to know that in a couple of months to a couple of years, you'll still have that money you put away, and maybe a bit more (to cover inflation), for a little holiday, a deposit on a house or car, or perhaps just in case of an emergency.

So, you choose to deposit it in a bank, and you earn a bank deposit rate. If you're wanting to do a bit better than a bank deposit, you need to put it into a money market fund, which has good liquidity.

> A **MONEY MARKET FUND** is generally considered a safe investment. It is a fund, managed by a professional manager, that grows monthly. The return on this fund can be reinvested or paid out to the investor.

Good liquidity means you can withdraw your money at short notice without incurring penalties. You get the yield pick-up (you earn a bit more than a simple cash deposit), as the professional fund manager pools your money with that of other people and takes a little more risk on your behalf.

When you're investing, you're looking further into the future. Investments are generally long term. That's when you take the money you've saved and add more risk in the hope that you can enhance your returns. By the time you've finished reading this book, you'll have a good handle on the concept of risk.

If you're close to retirement and it's an income you need to replace (that is, you are investing money in the knowledge that you will need to withdraw a monthly amount), then an income fund is best for you.

> As the name suggests, an **INCOME FUND** aims to pay the investor a high level of monthly income while maintaining a relatively stable initial capital base. The aim is to achieve higher than money market returns.

We're slowly moving up what finance professionals call the 'risk curve'. This starts with cash or cash deposits in a bank or money market account, and peaks with shares in companies, whether listed or unlisted. Apart from the possibility of lower returns, there are two reasons why shares are a riskier investment: first, there is a chance that the value of the shares you invest in will go to zero, and, second, the volatility of shares can play havoc with your plans, especially if you need to withdraw money for emergencies.

We have gone from bank deposits, which are considered low risk, to shares, which are considered high risk, in a heartbeat, but we'll return to all of these tools soon and explain in greater detail what comes in between.

> **PERSONAL INVESTMENT RISK** encompasses a host of scenarios that are linked to your not having enough money at the time that you need it, for example when you want to retire, or when the current value on your investment is lower than you had hoped (or than the initial amount you invested).
>
> **INVESTMENT RISK** is the acceptance of the possibility that a fund will not meet its investment-return targets.

While we make our way through the risk/return spectrum, remember this: investing is the ultimate goal, and investing is a long-term plan because markets are volatile and the effect of compounding is a wonderful wealth creator. Compounding is the ability to earn interest on interest already earned. We'll look more at the miracle of compounding in Chapter 8.

While we're busy building wealth, we also have short-term needs – buying a car, putting down a deposit on a house, paying school fees. For this reason, we also need to consider saving, because even though stock markets have historically generated higher returns than bank deposit rates, unfortunately for us, stock markets do not always go up.

The graph below shows the JSE All Share Index annual returns from 1974 to 2017. The All Share Index is a benchmark made up of all listed shares on the Johannesburg Stock Exchange (JSE), taking into account company values and weighted according to the values of other listed companies. Note that the annual average return per annum is 19,4%, but also note the exceptional return in 1979 of 94,4% and the very depressing two years of -18,9% and -23,2% in 1975 and 2008, respectively.

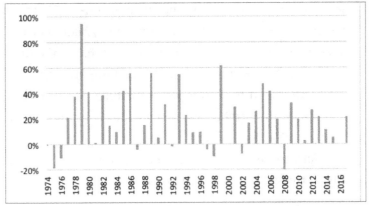

JSE All Share Index annual returns, 1974–2107

Source: Author's own, data from Bloomberg

We'd all love to have been invested in 1979 and to have avoided 2008, but none of us has a crystal ball or a time machine. In truth, the years that really bother people like me are the sequential years of 1995 (8,8%), 1996 (9,4%), 1997 (-4,5%) and 1998 (-10%); in my world, a couple of years of no cumulative growth is essentially a flat market.

Those same numbers, viewed cumulatively, look like this:

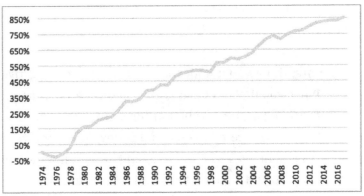

JSE All Share Index, cumulative returns, 1974–2017

Source: TradingEconomics.com

Seen over the longer term, the steep decline of 23,2% in 2008 looks more like a shallow pothole on the road to investment success, unless 1) you were never invested in the market – in which case it's your big missed opportunity – or 2) you were forced to withdraw your money at the end of 2008 and your investment was down a quarter (25%) on the previous year's calculation.

Now let's compare what would have happened if you had simply put your money in a bank deposit account. Look at the graph below:

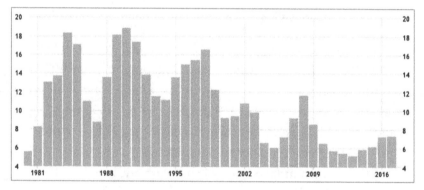

South African deposit interest rates, 1980–2017

Source: TradingEconomics.com

The first thing you'll notice is that there are no negative years. What you'll also notice is that there are no years of 94% returns; in fact, there is nothing over 19%. Between 1980 and 2017, the average rate you could get by depositing your money in a bank was 10,8% – reaching an all-time high of 18,86% in 1990 and a record low of 5,15% in 2013.

If you're trying to decide which of the two graphs you prefer, then you are beginning to understand the risk/return spectrum and how it applies to you. It is generally accepted that the younger you are, the more risk you can take, because there is less chance you will need your money when markets are flat or negative. As we get older, we want less risk because we are getting closer to retirement and do not want to have to withdraw our pensions when the markets are producing negative returns.

Setting personal finance goals

The disciplines of saving and investing start with a mindset check. Your attitude to money will determine your success rate: you must take responsibility for your finances; no one else will be coming to your rescue.

One of the fundamentals of success in almost anything you do in life is that you need to spend a relatively short amount of time planning for it. Even if things don't work out as planned, you at least have a goal and a path that you can get back to when you are thrown off course.

Financial freedom – or, better yet, financial independence – is no different. You're not going to get anywhere if you do not plan. Investment planning starts with identifying your life goals: do you want to study, buy a house, marry, have children, start your own business, become financially independent, retire well? For all of these goals, you need money.

Some of your goals will be short-term, some medium, and some long-term. Take pen to paper and make a list of your goals. Next to each goal, decide how much money you will need. You have a fair idea what a new wardrobe will cost, or what you want to spend on a new car. If you change your mind, you can always adjust these numbers. For retirement, it is a bit harder, but assume you want to live the same life-style you are living now. The general practice is to take your current salary and multiply it by 17 to give you a very rough estimate of how much you need in retirement. I also hope you will have no debt repayments to worry about in retirement. It's going to seem an unattainable number, but don't worry, you're reading this book to find out how you can reach that goal.

Hopefully, as you progress through this book, you will be able to 'guesstimate' more accurately how long you will need to save and invest to reach your goals. Chances are that each goal will require a slightly different strategy and length of time, and you need to understand which investment or savings products will best suit each of your goals.

Most people have similar short-, medium- and long-term financial goals:

Short-term goals	Medium-term goals	Long-term goals
New wardrobe	Paying off the car	Comfortable retirement
Deposit for a car	Paying off the house	Creating wealth
Deposit for a house	School fees	
Holiday	University fees	

Now make a list of your goals:

Short-term goals	Medium-term goals	Long-term goals

Without knowing you, there is one thing I can guarantee, and that is that your goals and your investment requirements will change. But that's fine, this book will give you hints on how to change your investment strategy as you progress through life.

Achieving your goals: the discipline of budgeting

Benjamin Franklin is also credited with saying, 'Beware of little expenses; a small leak will sink a great ship.' The first step to achieving your personal finance goals and becoming financially independent lies in taking control of your expenses. As with a small leak on a ship, a small leak in a budget can have terrible long-term consequences for any wealth-creation plan.

A water leak is relatively easy to detect. Those little expenses, however, are much more elusive, as they are most likely invisible. Financial leaks come about when you justify expenses by saying, 'It's such a small amount, I'm not going to miss it', 'It's not going to have a material impact on my overall wealth-creation plan' or 'It's too much effort to account for all the small expenses'. But beware: these small amounts add up. However, there is a solution to this challenge. It's called 'budgeting'.

Budgets give us a firm boundary of what is an acceptable amount to be spent on small items, and thus the ability to keep ourselves in check. It's simply a way of taking control. Here are some easy-to-implement ways of taking control of your budget:

1. *Get all your financial statements directed to one place* (normally in an email) and make sure you can easily access them when needed.

2. *Compare bank charges* – I can almost guarantee that you'll be shocked.

3. *Use only one card.* With one card, you can easily reconcile your income and your expenses. I would recommend finding out which bank card (debit or credit) is the cheapest. There is a particular issue to be aware of here: credit cards carry ridiculously high interest rates on outstanding balances. If you are going to purchase on credit, be aware of the full implications of taking on this kind of debt. I cannot stress this enough. I like using a credit card, because the transaction charges are minimal – but that's how they trap you. It's easy not to pay back the full outstanding amount at the end of the month, and any outstanding debit balance is likely to cost you dearly (on average 20% more than just paying cash for your purchases).

4. *Step away from store cards!* Like the credit card, buying goods on store credit is easy, but it comes loaded with expensive debt. Again, some store cards will offer you interest-free periods. It's a psychological trap, though. Not

because they are lying to you, or cheating you, but because it's easy not to repay the store card in full within the allocated period, and then the high interest rates kick in. If you must use a store card, then do your homework: find out the interest rate you are being charged and calculate how much more that item will cost you.

5. Also, be wary when stores offer 'three months free' where you buy an item on credit today and only start paying in three months. This only means that they will charge an exorbitant interest rate, insurance on the credit you take with them and a sweet delivery charge. Some might say this is a moot point, because consumers need to educate themselves and it's not the store's fault. Take the time to look for the loopholes in these 'specials'. By the time you've read the sections on compound interest and amortisation in Chapter 8, you should be sufficiently equipped to easily figure out how much interest you'll pay on loans like these.

6. *Be savvy about your choices* and the financial impact they have, and always be mindful of hidden costs. I learned this particular lesson again when I went shopping during the January sale season. I needed work clothes, so I bought a pair of trousers, a pair of shoes and three tops – five items in all, but not a single one of them was on sale. Then I saw a lovely sleeveless suit top with a pretty little frill on the collar and just one classy button with an elastic loop to hook into. There was only one size medium in the shop, but the elastic loop was broken. So, being the brave, money-savvy shopper that I am, I took it to the counter and asked the assistant to give me a discount. I would fix the loop

myself. Without blinking, she said, 'The discount is only 5%'. That's ridiculous, I thought. I expected at least 10%. So I got her to find a perfect top at another store. Now, if I want that top, I have to drive an additional ten kilometres and wander around a shopping centre; I hate shopping and shopping centres at the best of times. Ten minutes to sew the loop back myself versus petrol, time and frustration . . . I still laugh at my stupidity!

7. *Build a budget and use it religiously.* Start by keeping a monthly budget. I hate administrative work, so rather than inputting all the data at the end of each month, I update it whenever I have a spare minute during the day. It's just less daunting that way.

Keep in mind that some expenses are fixed; they recur regularly and are roughly the same amount each month. Other expenses, such as groceries and entertainment, vary on a monthly basis and fall into a broad category. The final amount spent on that category depends on many smaller decisions you make. Big, infrequent expenses that are hard to predict in advance include repairs to your car or your home. Big expenses that should be planned for include school fees.

Your budget is a most powerful tool. First, it gives you an instant snapshot of your financial life, and, second, it helps you to control your financial life. Your budget should list all your expenses, divided into fixed expenses and variable expenses. Your fixed expenses remain the same throughout the year, and include the following:

- Rent or mortgage payment
- Medical aid
- Insurance
- Rates and taxes
- Loan repayments
- TV subscriptions

Variable expenses include:
- Groceries
- Transport (fuel, taxi fares, toll fees)
- Telephone
- Transaction (banking fees)
- Clothing

For most people, the income line on their budget consists of a single salary. In the expenses category, you can refine your budget as much as you want; the more refined the categories, the better the control. Take your bank statement, have a look at each item and give it a 'home' in your budget. Your monthly grocery shopping is a living expense, but your daily R25 (or more) cup of 'branded' coffee is a luxury!

Be pedantic about reviewing the money you're spending every month. List as much as you can without making it a mammoth task that will put you off doing it regularly. You really need to do your budget every single month, or at least until you have cut out the excesses and have a handle on where the leaks are. I'd say six months is a fair amount of time for you to figure out where the leaks are. Depending on how disciplined you are, it may take another six to twelve months to plug them.

And another thing: there's no point in cheating. Admit to yourself how much money you've wasted each month!

You've got this. All it's going to take is a bit of discipline to identify and plug those leaks. In the budgeting process, you will soon find out where money is being wasted. Paying interest when it is not absolutely necessary is another waste of good money.

Large parts of this book were written at a restaurant called So-Yum in Hyde Park shopping centre in Johannesburg (I am very grateful to the staff for looking after my culinary needs and not judging me for the bad habit of typing while eating). It was here that I had the most inspiring talk with one of the managers, Gary. One day, I asked him if he knew the interest rate on his credit card. Without hesitation he told me he didn't, but he also explained that although he used to be a credit-card junkie, he'd managed to turn things around. Two years previously, he had decided to cut up all his store cards and keep only one credit card. The sacrifice was not small, but the glee with which he told me this story showed his delight at taking control of his finances.

In the same week we had the chat, Gary and his husband had just returned from an overseas holiday. Even though he was 'complaining' about how he needed to save for another overseas holiday, planned to coincide with a family wedding, I could tell he knew that they could afford it, and that he would enjoy it because he was proud of the fact that he had very little unnecessary debt. By foregoing the beautiful furniture and fancy dinners he'd previously splurged on using credit, he was now able to afford overseas trips. Gary took pleasure in telling me that if you zero your credit card, you don't pay interest. He now moves his salary directly into his credit card on payday and saves on interest.

It was not an easy two years, but Gary says that they are living the same lifestyle as before, and that the two years of sacrifice was worth it because the extra money he saves from paying interest can buy so much more. Gary and his husband also recently bought a new house, so they're not exactly debt-free. But we are now talking about how to make the transition from being mainly debt-free to investing the money he saves by not having unnecessary debt. Small steps; big dreams.

I am often asked whether it makes sense to save while you have debt. This pertinent question comes up often, especially as banks are likely to charge you more interest on your loan than you can achieve by investing the money in a low-risk portfolio. Considering that most people have debt, I don't believe the answer is straightforward.

Some debt can be considered 'crucial'. As much as I'd prefer not to buy a car with debt, I am aware that a car loan may be a necessity for most people. Few people will have enough money to purchase a house for cash, and therefore need to take on mortgage debt. It is worth realising that debt on a rental property is often considered a tax write-off for the landlord against the income generated from letting, and that this leverage is part of the attraction for property investors.

'Non-crucial' debt would then include credit and store cards, as well as personal loans. Make a plan to take control of these, but do not forego saving and investing, especially into investments such as pension funds that benefit significantly from the miracle of compounding.

There are a number of life situations that require you to have an emergency fund: out-of-medical-aid expenses, a new exhaust for your car, a broken geyser, etc. If you are unable to cover these with cash from your savings, then you are likely to try and access the first and likely most expensive debt you can. Unless you can access *low-interest* debt when you need it and know that you can pay it off at the end of the month, I suggest that you save enough money to create an emergency fund. Only you know how big or small your emergency fund needs to be, but my advice is to put it into a low-risk investment (cash or money market) to access even if you do have debt.

KEY POINTS

1. Decide on your short-, medium- and long-term goals.

2. Take control of your finances by budgeting.

3. Figure out what interest rate you are paying on your debt and get rid of as much debt as possible, starting with the loans that have the highest interest rates.

3

Clever in your thirties, relaxed in your sixties

A vital reason why you should save and invest is so you will be able to retire comfortably. According to the National Treasury, a mere 6% of South Africans will retire with enough money to enjoy the same standard of living they enjoyed while they were earning a salary.

In the exercise of listing your short-, medium- and long-term goals in the previous chapter, you would have added retirement under long-term goals. Research suggests that a capital sum of 17 times an individual's final annual salary, before tax, will produce an income equal to approximately 75% of the last salary if the individual retires at age 65. A couple of years ago, the figure was 11 times, but because we are living longer, we need more money. If we keep the age of retirement at 65, there is a good chance we will live longer in retirement without a salary than the years we worked. Some institutions are even suggesting that the first person to live to 200 has already been born (to which one financial institution responded with the clever tagline, 'How do you plan for that?').

In practical terms, if you are earning R1 million a year at retirement, you will need R17 million in investments when you retire. In order to achieve the 17-times target, you will need to contribute between 11% and 13% of your monthly salary, your salary needs to increase with inflation on an annual basis, and you need to earn a return of 3% to 5% above inflation – that's right, *above inflation*.

The table below will help you figure out if you are on target to have 17 times your salary at retirement. If you have been working for five years, you should have 1,2 times your annual salary in your pension fund or other investments; if you have been working for ten years, you need to have 2,3 times your annual gross salary in your pension fund or investments (we'll talk later about whether pension funds or discretionary investments are more tax-efficient).

Number of years worked	Multiple of current salary you should have saved
5	1,2 times
10	2,3 times
15	3,7 times
20	5,3 times
25	7,2 times
30	9,4 times
35	12 times
40	15 times

I have to emphasise that these calculations are based on the assumption that you will have paid off all your debt and kicked the children out of the house by the time you retire, and will travel less and cut down on luxuries. I understand that every individual has different goals, risk tolerances, earning power and demands on their income. Someone who works in a corporate job may have very different cash flow from an entrepreneur. And yet the goal is the same – to retire comfortably.

In October 2018, the Mercer Melbourne Global Pension Index[5] revealed that South Africa's pension system is not sustainable because it does not cover enough people and does not pay a decent income – and they were talking about the private pension pot. Just think how difficult it must be for people who are dependent on the government's pension grant of R1 600 a month.

There's so much to consider when planning your life, and you must also heed the immortal words of the poet Robert Burns: 'The best laid schemes o' Mice an' Men, Gang aft agley'.[6] In a nutshell, even the best planning does not guarantee a successful outcome.

A while ago I was on my bicycle, struggling up a hill, when an elderly gentleman came peddling alongside me and started making light conversation.

'This is great,' he said, 'I've found someone who cycles at my speed.'

He proceeded to tell me that, similar to me, he was making a comeback to cycling (me to triathlon), and that he hadn't cycled for three years because he was recovering from cancer, first lymphoma and then melanoma. But he had been tested a couple of weeks previously and was now in complete remission.

'Wow,' I replied breathlessly, 'that's great news, and you're already on your bike and challenging me on the hills.'

'Sure,' he said, 'I feel great, but I have to go back to work now, at the age of 72, because the medical treatment wiped out all my savings.'

He told me he had been a marketing consultant, and I couldn't help but wonder who was going to employ him in a country where the official unemployment rate is 27%, the unofficial rate is closer to 40%, and youth unemployment has reached over 50%. How was he going to fund the rest of his life? With good cause, he was worried.

His father had passed away when he was a young boy, but his uncles on both sides of the family had longevity in their favour. One of them had died only a couple of years before, at the age of 98. If that was going to be him, he would need another 26 years' worth of savings just to live, and since he'd already had cancer, twice, his medical aid premiums were over R5 000 per month.

He sped up the hill, leaving me only a little depressed. I like to think I'm relatively healthy, and I have a penchant for jokingly telling anyone who will listen how the women in my family outlive the men – not simply by a couple of years, but by decades. I comfort myself with the fact that I love what I do and will do it for as long as I am able, but there are so many 'what ifs' that it's hard to contemplate them all and plan for the future. But, I can't let being overwhelmed stop me from planning.

In this chapter I will show you how you can become less dependent on a pension system that doesn't pay a decent income. I will show you how you can avoid being one of the 94% of South Africans who will not have enough money to live comfortably after they lock their office door for the last time.

Here's some good news to bear in mind: if your investments return 12,5% per annum, you will double your money every six years. Consistency and time really are your friends when it comes to investing: the notional difference between someone who starts investing at age 20, invests R500 per month, increases their investment by 5% every year, and gets an average return of 15% per annum to retire at age 65, compared to someone who starts investing at age 30, is an astonishing R17 million. That's right, the person who started investing at 20 will have close to R23 million, while the person who started at age 30 will have just over R5,5 million.

And here's a bit more 'mathemagics': if they retire at the age of 70, simply delaying by a mere five years, the person who started investing at age 30 will have R11,5 million, while the person who started investing at age 20 will have accumulated R46,5 million. It's not even mathemagics, it's simply giving yourself the benefit of time and letting the impact of compound interest play out.

Your options at retirement

Imagine for a moment that you have decided to retire, and that you have managed to accumulate a notional amount of money in your pension and/or provident (retirement) fund. Because you will no longer be contributing to your retirement fund, you need to decide how to invest this money.

In South Africa, we have a couple of options when it comes to retirement investments. At the age of 55, you can cash in your retirement fund without too many tax implications and buy one of a number of annuities. Don't do it if you don't need to; as you may already have figured out, I will try to persuade you to work past 65 years of age if you have the option.

When you are ready to retire and cash out your retirement fund, you would be well advised to buy an annuity that will pay you a monthly stipend to replace your salary. You could trust your investment acumen and invest the money yourself or you could buy one of the kinds of annuities I list below.

> **ANNUITIES** are funds that insurance companies have put together that will pay you a monthly pension (stipend).

You have several options when it comes to annuities:

1. *Level annuity:* At first glance, this appears to be the cheapest option. The insurance company takes the notional money you have accumulated and calculates how long it will last (based on actuarial tables of mortality, i.e. life expectancy). They will then quote you a monthly stipend (pension payout). The level annuity offers a set amount per month, with no increase. Because there is no annual increase in payout amount, the initial amount tends to compare favourably with the other options. As tempting as it sounds to take the higher payout, don't rush your decision.

2. *Inflation-linked annuity:* This option is fairly self-explanatory; the insurance company will quote you an initial monthly payout amount that increases every year with inflation. That sounds like a good option, because the one thing you do have to worry about, and to negate at all costs, is an unpredictable rate of inflation (especially in emerging

markets like ours) because it quietly eats away at your spending (purchasing) power.

3. *With-profit annuity:* This is the uncertain option. Here, the insurance company quotes an initial monthly pension amount, and the annual increase is dependent on the company's profit declaration. The annual increase could be above or below inflation; in fact, it could be well above (and also well below) inflation, making this also an uncertain option. As you read this, you might be grabbing your phone to research how much profit insurance companies make. If you're going to do that exercise, let me remind you that historical performance is not an indicator of future performance.

4. *Living annuity:* This option has become popular in recent years. Based on inputs and a model, which your financial advisor should be happy to provide, you can choose the amount you want to withdraw every month. One of the reasons for the popularity of living annuities is that, on the death of the pensioner, any balance not withdrawn will be paid out to an elected beneficiary – which is not the case with the other annuity options. The possible negative outcome of this option is that if you withdraw too large a monthly sum, you can eventually run out of money. The key is to do your homework and be disciplined about living within your means.

In Chapter 2 we compared the graphs of the JSE All Share Index and the rates of returns on bank deposits. Despite shares being more volatile, the overall long-term return was almost double that of the rate of interest we were getting on bank deposits over the same period, but deposits offered stability of capital (lower risk). Shares returned an average of 19,4% but included years when the market fell 18,9% and 23,2%. Bank deposits returned 10,8% on average per annum but there were no negative months.

Shares are often known as 'equities', and for our purposes the two terms are more or less interchangeable.

> **STOCKS/SHARES/EQUITIES** refer to ownership in a company. If the company has issued 100 shares and you own ten shares, you effectively own 10% of the company. The value of shares listed on stock exchanges fluctuates daily, as will the value of your share portfolio. Owning a share in the company generally means you have the right to vote at annual general meetings (AGMs) and you will be the recipient of any cash distributions the company may make (dividends).

While being invested in the higher-risk equity (share) market offers a higher rate of return over the longer term, lower-risk money-market-style funds offer lower returns, but with the benefit of stability of capital.

With the above options in mind, I note that pensioners tend to make the risk-averse decision, and understandably so. They've worked hard to accumulate capital, and their natural tendency is to protect that capital. There are two key factors that come into play here:

- The amount of money you have accumulated
- How much money you need to withdraw every month

If you are likely to live for 20 to 30 years after retirement, and you need your monthly withdrawals to increase by inflation every year, you will need an investment that consistently returns, at minimum, the rate of inflation. The only way to attain an above-inflation return is by being invested in equities. The question is, how much of your portfolio needs to be invested in this high-risk asset class?

If you need to withdraw 2% to 3% from your living annuity every year, you can keep your equity exposure at a relatively low 30% to 35%. This equation gives you 30 to 40 years of living off your annuity.

If you increase your income drawdown slightly to between 5% and 6%, the equity exposure you need to take on increases significantly to between 70% and 75% in order to get to the end of your life before getting to the end of your money.

Your appetite for volatility can be an important determinant of whether or not you will achieve your financial goal. Being cautious and trying to minimise volatility or big short-term losses in your portfolio may not necessarily be the best option for you.

If you've decided you can afford to draw 5% of your living annuity, and you invest 75% of your portfolio in shares, there is a 10% chance that you may not meet your target, that is, have enough money to the end. If, however, you invest only up to 40% in equities (shares) the likelihood of failure increases to 50%. You need the higher returns associated with equities to make it, despite the short-term volatility that comes with this asset class.

A common mistake investors make is to think that the less volatile money market funds, which offer near-certain yields, will be sufficient. Sure, the money market fund may offer a higher return than your drawdown. However, if the money market yield is 6,5% and you are drawing down only 4%, simplistically it would appear that you have 2,5% extra. But what hasn't been factored into that equation is inflation. And unfortunately, money market funds rarely beat inflation.

To grow your investment by more than inflation, you must be invested not only in a money market fund but also in the equity market, despite the fact that this comes with higher volatility. When we design your portfolio, we will look at funds that offer returns of inflation plus anything between 3% and 7%.

Although you may not like risk, it will become apparent that you will have to stomach a fair amount of risk (while not overextending yourself) in order to reach your financial goals.

Avoid withdrawing your pension fund

When you change jobs, you have the option to withdraw from your pension fund. Do NOT do it. It's widely believed that millennials (those born between 1981 and 1996) will change jobs more often than any generation that has gone before them and are most at risk of retiring without sufficient capital because they will be tempted to withdraw their pension benefits. I understand that there are circumstances that may require the cash you suddenly have access to, and I'm no stranger to thinking I could use that money better somewhere else, but here are some things you must consider. When you're in your twenties, retirement seems so far away, and there are many more important things to do with your money. In your thirties and forties, you know retirement is coming, but you'll tell yourself that you have better uses for the money than growing it slowly in a pension fund.

But here's a wake-up call: to reach the same comfortable retirement, someone who starts investing in their twenties will have to save approximately 12,5% of their salary. To reach the same retirement goal, someone who starts saving in their thirties will have to save almost a quarter of their salary. If someone starts saving only in her forties, she will have to contribute more than 40% of her salary. At this stage, it gets far too onerous to even think about withdrawing your retirement savings. In addition, the tax implications of withdrawing your money before retirement are not in the investor's favour.

If you have an RA, you will have access to your money at the age of 55. Despite my assertion that it is not a good idea to withdraw your money, there are in fact three scenarios in which you can withdraw the money. The first is if you have less than R7 000 in your fund and you are no longer contributing. The second is if you emigrate financially, although this option is taxable as per the table below.

Taxable income (R)	Rate of tax (R)
0–25 000	0% of taxable income
25 001–660 000	18% of taxable income above 25 000
660 001–990 000	114 300 + 27% of taxable income above 660 000
990 001 and above	203 400 + 36% of taxable income above 990 000

The third scenario is if you are permanently disabled, which is seen as early retirement. In this instance, the rules are that you can withdraw the full amount if you have less than R247 500 saved, or you can take one third in a lump sum, and the rest must be used to purchase one of the annuities we spoke about above. For this scenario, the following tax rates apply:

Taxable income (R)	Rate of tax (R)
0–R500 000	0%
R500 001–R700 000	18% of taxable income above R500 000
R700 001–R1 050 000	R36 000 + 27% of taxable income above R700 000
R1 050 001 and above	R103 500 + 36% of taxable income above R1 050 000

Once you get to retirement, make a point of understanding your options and choose wisely the amount you wish to draw down every month and which post-retirement investment you wish to make. Your plan should be to avoid ending up as one of the 94% of South Africans who retire with insufficient funds.

KEY POINTS

1. Start planning your retirement early.
2. Take advantage of the substantial tax benefits of a retirement fund.
3. Understand your four options at retirement and which annuity suits you (level annuity, inflation-linked annuity, with-profit annuity or living annuity).

4

Your friend, the stock market

I simply love the stock market. Why? The stock market doesn't care what skin colour, age or gender I am. In fact, she is oblivious of my physical appearance. She cares only that I do my homework and remain a loyal investor. And through all her ups and downs, in the end she rewards me handsomely.

Those rewards are tangible, and I can prove it. Let's start with the mathematical fact that with a 12,5% return per year, every six years she will double my money. It's not 'mathe-magics', it's just compound interest (which is a bit like magic).

The stock market is, very simply, a regulated environment and platform where people can buy and sell securities. Securities include shares of companies and derivatives on those shares.

> **DERIVATIVES** are investment instruments that, for a small fee, will give you the equivalent of exposure to a share. You do not have to own the share to take advantage of the return (negative or positive) on a derivative. For example: if you paid a small fee (normally between 1% and 5% of the share price) to the seller of a call option (a type of

derivative), you don't own the share, but any movement in the share price above the agreed share price will mean you are entitled to the profit up to the agreed expiry date of the call option. If the share decreases in value or does not increase in value at the expiry date of the option, you have only lost the small amount you paid for the option.

Securities also include baskets of shares and a few other things, including commodities such as gold, platinum, crude oil and wheat. There was a time when you could even trade pork bellies. I didn't just throw in pork bellies to check if you were concentrating; up until 2011 you really could trade pork bellies! According to Investopedia.com (bookmark it!), pork bellies are a key ingredient in a lot of meat products, and the trading of pork-belly futures was a way for 'meat packers to hedge the volatile pig market'.[7] This meant that they would buy the pork bellies at a specified price that appealed to them, and then sell a similar amount for delivery in the future to ensure the profit margin remains consistent.

Along with hedging out the volatile prices of commodities, the point of having a stock market is to give companies a place to raise capital. Companies raise capital by selling shares in their companies or by borrowing money from investors. Then they use that money to grow their companies.

Why don't they just borrow from the bank? That's because banks, believe it or not, can be expensive and are risk-averse. They actually want their money back and don't really care what your cash flow looks like when that money is due. So, the company comes to you and me, the investors (or lenders) – who can be either professional or amateur investors – to raise money. Of course, there is usually the promise that they will grow our money.

Let's assume you are an investor and have bought shares in a company, or have loaned money to a company, and the time has come when you want that money back. It doesn't often happen that the company is ready to buy those shares back from you or to repay the money you loaned them. This is when you need other investors who are willing to buy those shares from you or to take over the loan, hopefully at a profit to you, and still with more potential upside (the possibility to make more profit) for the next investor. We're going to ignore losses for now, and just talk about an instance where you may well forego the total profit you could have made for the liquidity (cash) you require as soon as possible.

Very sneakily, I've just introduced you to primary and secondary markets. The primary market was when the company sold the shares to you (or you loaned them money, at an attractive interest rate), and the secondary market is when you sold those same shares (or the loan).

In a nutshell, this is what happens on the stock market every day. Companies go to the stock market to raise capital to expand their businesses, and investors buy and sell shares or loans to make a profit by backing the listed company's growth potential. The basic premise really is that simple.

Almost every day of the year, there is a stock market open and trading somewhere in the world, with traders, asset managers, stockbrokers or direct investors buying and selling securities (shares and loans and other clever products).

Since the mid-1980s stock exchanges have been converted to electronic/computerised trading. Before that, the system was known as 'open outcry'. In an open-outcry system, traders gather around their trading posts on the trading floor wearing colour-coded or patterned tunics, which identify the company they work for or their asset-class speciality (such as bonds, shares and commodities).

Imagine for a few seconds the following scene: Elon Musk tweets the successful launch of Tesla's (share code: TSLA) first electric car and the price of crude oil tumbles $5 a barrel to $50/barrel, because we all know that with the advent of electric cars, the demand for petrol will decrease and traders are pre-empting the drop in demand.

An oil trader, in his black-and-gold-striped jacket stands at his post and thinks that the dawn of the electric car will be the death knell for oil.

He shouts, gesticulating wildly, 'Sell!' with his palms facing outward, pushing his hands away from his body.

'Nine!' with four fingers pointing sideways, parallel to the floor, at chin level.

'Thousand!' with three fist bumps on his forehead (bumps represent ten, hundred, thousand).

'Fifty!' with five fingers on the chin, followed by one fist bump on his forehead.

The trader is selling 9 000 barrels of Brent Crude oil at $50 per barrel.

A second oil trader on the floor thinks that this move in oil is overdone (fallen too much). This could be a great buying opportunity and it won't last long, so he needs to hurry. Determined to get noticed and heard over the din of a hundred other traders, he shouts: 'Buy!' with palms facing inward and making a pulling gesture.

'Fifty!' with open hand, all five fingers at chin level, followed by a single fist bump to the forehead.

'Six!' with one finger, parallel to the floor at chin level.

'Thousand!' with three fist bumps to the forehead.

His $300 000 trade is complete – 6 000 barrels of oil change hands at $50 per barrel. The deal is written on the massive chalk board above the trading pit, pieces of paper will be exchanged, and trades will eventually be settled.

I've simplified it a bit, but you get the idea of the noise, the fast pace, the enormous room for error – and, oh, the adrenaline rush. There are still a few open-outcry exchanges today, such as the Chicago Mercantile Exchange (CME), and the Chicago Board of Trade, where they trade commodity futures and options (including lean hog futures and soybean futures).

The JSE, which was previously known by its full name of Johannesburg Stock Exchange, was started one year after gold was discovered on the Witwatersrand. The Johannesburg Exchange & Chambers Company was established by a London businessman, Benjamin Minors Woollan, and out of this was born the JSE on 8 November 1887.

I recently had a meeting with a potential client in the centre of Johannesburg. Their offices are in Sauer Street in the Johannesburg CBD, and as I walked into the entrance of the building, I spotted an old 'green' board – the green board on which they wrote the prices of shares in chalk – preserved as a monument to the old way of trading.

Today we see numbers on a screen, and the numbers change by the second. I can only imagine the pace of the scribe, spending the entire day writing up numbers, rubbing them out, being shouted at, rewriting the new numbers, waiting for that bell to ring at the end of the day when he is finally able to breathe as the last numbers stay on the board overnight.

The JSE's growth has been phenomenal. In 2017 67,8 million trades were completed, with a value of R5 479 432 878 000 (that's R5,4 trillion). That's a lot of activity, so thank goodness the JSE became an electronic exchange in the early 1990s. This means that we now buy and sell securities via our computers.

Imagine sitting at your desk with the JSE's trading page open on your screen. Right-click on the share code, up pops a small window, choose 'buy' or 'sell', input the number of shares you wish to trade, the price you wish to trade at, and voilà . . . if there is an opposite trader at your price, you're done! Not the same wild behaviour as during the days of the trading pits, but the expediency and size of trades with a slight margin of error will still give you a decent adrenaline rush.

In short, the stock market is where we go to invest and make our money grow. I've shown you the statistics; on average, the JSE has returned over 16% per annum for the last 20 years. Sure, the stock market is not the only place to grow your money, but think about the opportunity cost. If you are not invested in the stock market, you are losing out on 16% growth per annum.

If you have put your money somewhere else, such as in your brother's restaurant, in property or in your friend's new app, then you should be making more than 16% per annum to make it worth your while. As we progress on this investment journey, you will have the opportunity to compare different types of investments and asset classes, and make a call on which ones best suit you.

Global stock exchanges compared

There are many stock markets and approximately 20 major stock exchanges in the world, of which 19 (including South Africa) belong to the 'trillion dollar club', that is, they have market capitalisations of over $1 trillion. This means that the value of the shares listed on each of these exchanges adds up to over $1 trillion.

Some exchanges include stocks that are listed in more than one country. For example, our very own home-grown Anglo American mining company, which was founded in Johannesburg in 1917 by Sir Ernest Oppenheimer, and which is the world's largest platinum producer, has its primary listing in London and maintains secondary listings on the JSE, the SIX Swiss Exchange, the Botswana Stock Exchange and the Namibian Stock Exchange. On every exchange in the world, listed shares have a stock code. For Anglo American, the JSE stock code is AGL, in Switzerland it is AMM, in Botswana ANGLO (that's easy to remember), and in Namibia the code to trade is ANM.

Anglo American moved its main listing to the London Stock Exchange (LSE) from the JSE in May 1999 to improve its liquidity. (This is slightly different from my previous explanation of liquidity in your personal investments; in this case, liquidity refers to the volume of shares traded. The higher the number of shares, the better the liquidity.) One of the reasons companies list their shares is to gain access to capital, and the bigger the exchange (more trade/liquidity), the easier it is to access capital. By comparison the JSE-listed Anglo American shares trade on average $35 million dollars per day, while the London-listed shares trade on average $115 million per day.

By a significant margin, the New York Stock Exchange (NYSE) is the largest of the world's stock exchanges, with a market capitalisation of over $24 trillion. This is followed by another American exchange, the Nasdaq (an acronym for the National Association of Securities Dealers Automated Quotations), with a market capitalisation of approximately $10 trillion.

> **MARKET CAPITALISATION** is simply the number of shares issued by a company multiplied by the share price. If a company has 100 shares and today the share price is R10, the market capitalisation (often simply referred to as 'market cap') is R1 000. If tomorrow the share price falls to R9 per share, the market cap will be R900. The market cap of an exchange is all the company market caps added together; and as you know by now, the market cap changes by the millisecond.

You may be wondering why there are two major stock exchanges in one country (although there are often more than that). Here's why. Think of a stock exchange as a business, competing for the business of companies (because exchanges generate revenue by charging companies for the privilege of listing their shares) and for your business (because these same exchanges charge the investor for trading).

Granted, the barriers to entry are generally high for a stock-exchange business. Starting an exchange involves considerable capital expenditure, and requires compliance with national regulations, investment in computer systems, customer acquisition, cost competition, and so on. But it may well be a worthwhile business to get into, especially when you consider how much easier it is to trade and acquire customers in the digital world. In the 2017 financial year – and coincidentally its 130th anniversary – The JSE generated R2.2 billion in revenue (and that wasn't even its best year).

Some stock exchanges compete on price: for example, the NYSE charges up to $500 000 for a new listing and the same fee per annum, while the Nasdaq charges between $50 000 and $75 000 for a new listing and approximately $27 500 per annum. So why bother listing on the NYSE? Again, the reason is liquidity: the NYSE has almost three times as much trading as the Nasdaq, and provides greater access to capital and apparently better price discovery.

Share prices are driven by investor and trader sentiment (based on research) and their valuation of the company. I can guarantee that every investor and trader will have a different absolute value, or target price they think the share should be trading at. As investors, we try to predict what the share price will be in future, and there are so many variables. Some investors and traders may be happy to buy a share at R10, while others may sell at R9,50 and some may even think it's worth R20 a share. If the share trades a lot, then it is easy to buy and sell around market consensus. If the share doesn't trade that much, it will trade further away from consensus;

the more the share trades, the closer to consensus and the better price discovery.

The NYSE was founded in 1792 and is clearly more established than the Nasdaq, which was established in 1971. Shares that trade on the NYSE, such as ExxonMobil, General Electric and Bank of America, are perceived to be less volatile than shares traded on the Nasdaq, which hosts newer, technology-based companies such as Apple, Microsoft, Amazon, etc. In addition to the NYSE and the Nasdaq, there is also the American Stock Exchange, which was once the second-largest exchange after the NYSE.

Mostly, exchanges are registered by country, but some exchanges are regional and serve more than one country. Africa, for example, has two regional stock exchanges: the Bourse Régionale des Valeurs Mobilières (BRVM), headquartered in Abidjan, Côte d'Ivoire, which serves Benin, Burkina Faso, Guinea-Bissau, Côte d'Ivoire, Mali, Niger, Senegal and Togo; and the Bourse Régionale des Valeurs Mobilières d'Afrique Centrale (BVMAC), located in Libreville, Gabon. The BVMAC serves the Central African Republic, Chad, Democratic Republic of Congo, Equatorial Guinea and Gabon.

We have mainly spoken about stock exchanges, where shares in companies are traded, but there are also bond exchanges, and agriculture, commodity and derivative exchanges. The Bond Exchange of South Africa (BESA), founded in 1996, used to be independent until it was acquired by the JSE in 2009. It was responsible for regulating and trading interest-yielding products (bonds) and their derivatives.

> **BONDS** are loans made by the investor to a company. When a company needs capital, instead of issuing more shares, it can borrow money from the investors with an interest rate that is generally higher than bank deposits and a fixed term. The company, which is the borrower and is also known as the issuer, will set the repayment date and negotiate with banks and investors on the interest rate it has to pay. Fixed income is an asset class that pays regular, fixed interest (monthly, quarterly, semi-annually or annually) and bonds fit perfectly into this category.

The CME and the Chicago Board of Options Exchange, established in 1973 on the 125th anniversary of the Chicago Board of Trade, along with the New York Mercantile Exchange and Commodity Exchange, are probably the best-known derivatives exchanges.

It is difficult to know the exact size of the derivatives market because some derivatives are not traded on an exchange (banks deal directly with each other), but I have seen guesstimates in excess of a quadrillion US dollars, which are the two basic reasons for why Warren Buffett, in a 2002 letter to shareholders, called derivatives 'financial weapons of mass destruction'.[8]

It may interest you to know that the Mumbai-based National Stock Exchange of India Ltd (NSE), which was established only in 1992, is the second-largest derivatives trading exchange in the world, and in fact the largest single-stock futures trading platform in the world. It is also home to the Nifty 50 benchmark index, which is similar to the JSE All Share Index.

An **INDEX** is a mathematical measure of the stock market. In South Africa, the benchmark index, an index that measures the whole stock market, is called the FTSE JSE All Share Index (All Share or ALSI for short). The JSE also slices up the market into smaller sectors such as listed property shares, financial shares (or, even smaller, bank shares), mining sector, etc. The index itself is simply a mathematical equation and cannot be traded, but investors can buy products, such as ETFs, that replicate the index.

In a world where speed is of the essence, the LSE claimed in 2010 to be able to process trades at 124 microseconds. However, in 2012 the NSE claimed to have 'attained nirvana' by being able to process trades at the speed of light.[9]

Is the stock market a zero-sum game?

When you think that investors and traders are buying shares from each other, it would almost make sense that the stock market is a zero-sum game. The trader who buys low and sells high makes money, while the trader who sells low and buys high loses.

In fact, the market is not a zero-sum game. Trader 1 does not necessarily have to make money in order for Trader 2 to lose money, as they are buying and selling at different times and also buying and selling a variety of different instruments. In some cases, a specific trade may be zero-sum (particularly in derivative trades that are done directly between two traders, but even then there is likely to be an underlying hedge that allows for both to make money on the trade).

The market may not be a zero-sum game, but it has occasionally fallen sharply in what is known as a 'sell-off'. The massive drop on the US stock market on Black Tuesday (29 October 1929) is considered to have been the catalyst for the Great Depression, a worldwide economic slump whose effects lasted for 12 years. Shares began to fall on 24 October 1929 (Black Thursday), and finally hit bottom on 8 July 1932, having fallen 89% from peak to trough. It took the US stock market until November 1954 to completely recover the losses incurred over that three-year period. And yet, over the long term, the stock market has still delivered positive returns.

Every pessimist reading this will wonder whether it is worth taking the risk of losing 89% and waiting 25 years to recover that money, but I want to emphasise the fact that the Great Depression was not simply the result of an overheated stock market. The economic slump that followed the crash of 1929–1932 was the result of a complex interaction of factors, including over-extension of credit to consumers, increasing income inequality, growing trade protectionism, a collapse in agricultural prices (leaving farmers struggling) and massive drought in the American Midwest. Furthermore, although the US had boomed after the end of the First World War, European countries were unable to reboot their economies and were suffering a loss of confidence.

So, to say that the stock market was the cause of the Great Depression would be short-sighted, but the feverish trading in shares on the New York exchange was a clear indicator that the economy was about to turn – drastically. Between 1929 and 1932 the world's Gross Domestic Product (GDP) fell by approximately 15%. Compare that with the global financial crisis of 2008–2009, when global GDP was estimated to have fallen less than 1% and the US stock market fell 54% from its peak in October 2007.

How to buy your first shares

There are a multitude of options when investing on the stock market, and you don't have to know everything about it to start investing. Two of the most common options are unit trusts and exchange-traded funds (ETFs). (Unit trusts are covered in more detail in Chapter 5.)

> **UNIT TRUSTS** and **EXCHANGE-TRADED FUNDS (ETFs)** are portfolios of shares, bonds or property in which an asset manager makes the decision about which shares and bonds to buy and groups them into a portfolio or fund.

You can buy an ETF on the stock market (or stock exchange) – the words 'exchange traded' really gives it away. There are a number of well-known ETF providers on the JSE, for example Absa or CoreShares. You can access them through a stock-broking account, or on a platform such as EasyEquities or etfSA.

You may not have direct access to the stock market, as systems and licences are expensive and highly regulated, but you could easily buy and sell shares or ETFs on one of the banks' investing platforms. There's absolutely no reason not to open your own stockbroking account on these platforms. The banks' platforms are secure and there is little risk of insolvency, but they can be expensive. Their justification is that until recently, there has been little competition from other companies and the banks have had to spend money on building systems to enable the ordinary person to trade.

There are cheaper platforms, such as etfSA and Wealthport (for building your portfolio with ETFs) and EasyEquities (for share trading, RAs and tax-free savings accounts). etfSA is a simple, cost-effective website, and offers access to highly regarded ETF specialists, such as Nerina Visser and Mike Brown, who have both been in the industry for decades. I call Nerina 'Madame BettaBeta' because she developed the Betta-Beta product, which is aimed at giving individuals access to the entire market at low cost. These markets simply replicate, not do better than the market.

At time of writing, the minimum investment on etfSA was R300, and you can choose between a host of ETFs and bundle them into an RA or tax-free savings, which we cover in more detail in Chapter 10. EasyEquities is equally simple: the minimum investment is R100 and you have the option to buy a range of local and offshore products.

Your options for buying an ETF include shares, bonds and listed property. At this stage, you may not know your risk profile, and so if you are using this exercise as a way to help you understand how the market moves, I suggest you invest a small amount of money into an All Share ETF. Watch how the value of your ETF changes every day. Read articles on financial websites such as Moneyweb.co.za or Fin24.co.za. Even if you only read the headlines or the short stock market snapshot, you'll get a fair sense of what drives the market.

KEY POINTS:

1. Stock markets are where companies go to raise capital from investors.
2. Investors use stock markets to generate investment returns.
3. The simplest, cheapest and lowest-risk way for you to start your own investment portfolio and get to understand the vagaries of the market is to buy an ETF.

5

From shares to property – taking a closer look at asset classes

Your aim in investing is to end up with an investment portfolio made up not only of ETFs, but also some cash, local shares, bonds, property (physical property or listed property), offshore shares and bonds.

My friend Nerina Visser, or Madame BettaBeta, often compares building an investment portfolio to baking a cake. Before mixing the ingredients, you should first think about what type of cake you are going to bake.

Part of knowing what cake to bake is having a fairly good knowledge of the ingredients. While it might not be necessary to know what baking powder is made of, or what chemical process occurs when you use it, you should know that its purpose is to make the cake rise and give it a light, fluffy texture. You could use honey or sugar to make the cake sweeter, but you need to know which is better for the type of cake you are making.

This chapter will explain the different types of ingredients – or asset classes – that could potentially go into your investment portfolio cake. Once you know the impact each asset class will have on your portfolio, you can decide whether you would like to make a chocolate cake, a sponge cake, banana muffins or maybe a Black Forest gateau.

The main asset classes that people invest in are shares (equities), bonds (fixed-income) and cash (money market or bank deposits). Cash, shares in companies and bonds can be compared to the water, flour and dairy ingredients that most cakes require.

If the recipe asks for flour, the question is, do we want to use wheat flour or almond flour? In the context of building an investment portfolio, this means do we want to buy shares in mining companies or shares in IT companies? The choice between cow's milk or almond milk can be likened to government-issued bonds versus bonds issued by listed companies.

I've previously mentioned that companies go to the stock market to raise money to expand their operations and sometimes even to minimise debt. The question you need to ask yourself is, do I want to buy shares in a company, or do I want to lend them money? Each of these behaves differently. When you lend a company money, you will receive a regular interest payment that is defined upfront, and if all goes according to plan, you will receive your full capital back at the end of the term of the loan. In contrast, when you buy shares in a company, the share price will fluctuate every day and the company may or may not pay you a dividend, and they can decide at the end of their financial year how much of a dividend to pay.

> **DIVIDENDS** are payments to shareholders made out of the profits of the company. The company can choose to pay the dividend in cash or offer you more shares in the company to the equivalent value.

Just as shares and bonds behave differently, property and gold also behave differently. Ideally, you want to build a portfolio that has the basic ingredients (milk, eggs, flour), while choosing the specific ingredient (wheat flour or almond flour, or cow's milk or almond milk) that work well together.

Each ingredient in the cake represents a different asset class. By understanding the risk and return expectations associated with each asset class, we can match our investment goals to each of the asset classes and refine our investment strategy.

Investing is considered to be a risky business, and one of the things we will try to do when designing a portfolio that best suits you, will be to mitigate that risk. A wonderful tool to mitigate risk is diversification (from the verb to diversify, meaning 'to increase the variety'). Diversification is going to come up a lot in this chapter, so it's good to get a handle on it. However, to diversify, we need to understand what we are diversifying into. Luckily for us, similar assets (gold shares, property shares, bonds etc.) have a tendency to behave in a similar manner with regard to return and risk profiles.

It is generally accepted that higher returns can only be generated by taking higher risk. Shares in a company are a higher risk than a bond because, unlike bonds, there is no certainty of regular cash returns (interest payments versus dividend payments) and there is less certainty around the return of your capital when you sell the share, whereas with a bond you should get your full invested capital at the end of the term. Despite this uncertainty, historically, shares have produced higher returns. This is only an example of two different risk/return profiles, but each asset class has its own comparative risk return profile.

To keep things simple, I have tried to avoid using jargon or giving long definitions, but the subject of asset classes can get complicated. This chapter is about conveying the basics so that you know why you have chosen the asset, or combination of assets, you have. Knowing the asset classes and how you can make money out of them is the first step in designing an investment portfolio.

Shares/stocks/equity versus bonds

There's a reason why we call a share a share; if you own one, you own a share of someone's company. You may not have a say in the day-to-day running of the company, but it does mean you have the right to vote at annual shareholder meetings, and, more importantly, you share in the profits of the company through dividend payouts and in the growth of the company as its share price increases.

Here's a story most people know well, but I'm going to put an investor spin on it. On 1 April 1976 (yes, April Fool's Day!), Steve Jobs, Steve Wozniak and Ronald Wayne founded a company called Apple Computer Incorporated (later renamed Apple Inc). I'm sure you know that you need money to start a company. What most people do not know is that Jobs sold his VW bus for $750 and Wozniak sold his very special HP65 financial calculator for $500 to buy supplies to build their first prototype computer.

When they got their first order, they needed $15 000 to buy more supplies to fulfil the orders. No matter what we say in hindsight, I can guarantee that there are not many of us today who would have loaned these guys $15 000 – and nor was there at the time. I'm not sure whether Jobs was more hustler than charmer, but, either way, he convinced his supplier to give him enough product to fulfil the order (that is, to build computers) and afford them 30 days' credit. The young men built and delivered their first computers, got paid $25 000 by their customer and paid their supplier the outstanding $15 000 – all within the 30 days. That alone makes for a good story.

As the company grew, so did its cash requirements. Not only did they need more money for supplies, they also needed more money for research and development. And, for the record, they didn't always make the extraordinary sales and profits on the subsequent sales as they did on their first sale to Paul Terrell, founder of The Byte Shop, one of the first personal computer retailers.

By then, they could have gone to the bank – but, as you now know, banks don't like risk. Most banking institutions do not lend money to new businesses, which is why we have the proliferation of private equity companies. The private equity folks do their level best to spot the next big thing before it becomes that big thing – in other words, when shares in the company are still cheap.

Often, private equity companies will fund the start-up business through a combination of lending them money (bonds) and buying shares in the company. Investors sometimes prefer to take less risk and rather lend money to the company in the form of bonds. Another reason bonds issued by a company are less risky than shares in a company is because if the company goes bankrupt, the value of the shares goes to zero. However, bonds may still have a claim on the assets of the company (it is usually monetised through a fire sale).

So, a start-up company – in our example, Apple – issues a bond, which the lender buys. The issuer/seller promises to pay back the buyer of the bond (the lender) by a specified date at a given interest rate. The regular interest payments (also called coupons) are usually biannual, and the capital (initial amount loaned) is paid back on the specified date. Now you know how a bond works.

Between 1976 and 1980 Apple raised money from private equity companies a couple of times. But access to bonds is not limitless, and sometimes the founders of a company want to take some money off the table (monetise their profitable investments) by selling some or all of their shares in the company for cash, which they will use to pay themselves and expand the business. There is also the option of issuing more shares in the company and diluting current shareholders.

For example, if the company was valued at R100 000 and there were 100 shares in issue, each share is worth R1 000 (R100 000 ÷ 100). If the company needed another R10 000 it could issue another 10 shares and sell them. The company is still valued at R100 000 but there are now 110 shares in issue, and the value of each share is now R909,09 (R100 000 ÷ 110). Hopefully, the company will use the R10 000 to increase the value of the company.

For Apple, the time came at the end of 1980 when they were ready to list as a public company on the stock exchange (share code: AAPL); they chose the tech-heavy Nasdaq. Effectively, what they were doing was selling shares to Joe Public to raise money to expand the company and for the current shareholders (not only the founders, but also the private equity investor companies) to take some money off the table –

in other words, to unlock profit sitting on the private equity company's balance sheet. This meant that users of the company's products – first the Macintosh, followed later by the iPod, the iPhone, the MacBook Air and many others – were now also allowed to buy shares in the company.

There is something so very beautiful in the simplicity of owning a part of a company where you spend your money. Let's say you pay $100 for an iPod, and, for ease of understanding, let's say that $25 of that is profit for Apple. You could buy a cheaper MP3 player, but let's face it, there is something so aesthetically and intangibly appealing about the iPod.

Now imagine there was a way of getting back maybe $0,01 (just one US cent) of that $25 profit (that's 0,04%) – not at all exciting. Imagine you also got $0,01 of every iPod bought by your friends, family and colleagues. Or $0,01 of every iPod ever sold – by 2007 Apple had sold 100 million iPods. Take out your iPhone right now and do the calculation: 0,01 multiplied by 100 000 000 (the answer you see is US dollars, not cents).

I have simplified this example, so let me at least clarify this principle: as an investor, you do not always get paid out all of the profit of a company, but if you had bought $1 000 worth of Apple stock when they listed on the Nasdaq in December 1980, by December 2016 your investment would have been worth $300 505 – and that's excluding the $15 740 you would have received in dividends through the years. There are worse things you could have done with your money.

This is a near perfect risk/return example of an investment in shares versus bonds, because the risk taken in buying shares was worth it, as you made higher profits than if you were a bondholder.

More on shares and why we love dividends

When you own shares, not only do you have the right to attend the company's AGM, but, more importantly, you have the right to partake of the profits of the company through dividend payouts. While it's the company management's decision how much of the profit will be paid out or how much will be kept in the company to continue growing the business, you do get a vote at the AGM and sometimes that vote includes whether or not to change policy.

When you buy and sell shares, you are effectively deciding whether or not you think a particular company is a good one, whether you like and believe in its management team, if the economic environment favours the company, and, finally, whether you think the share price is going to go up or down.

Some people buy shares for capital growth, and some buy shares for dividend payouts. These goals are not mutually exclusive, but as you can imagine, when a company is still young, it will want to use all the available cash to grow the business, whether it's through research and development, buying assets or employing bigger teams, instead of paying out dividends. You can then expect the company to become more valuable and for its share price to rise. If that happens, you'll get the benefit in the growth of your capital, if not through dividend payouts.

Receiving a dividend is almost as much fun as seeing the price of the share you own go up. By paying a dividend, the company rewards you for being a shareholder through the year. But dividends are not a certainty (for that we buy real estate investment trusts). Dividends are paid out only if there is money left over after costs are covered, some debt is repaid, and the company doesn't need the cash to cover other expenses.

More often than not, companies pay dividends before paying down all the outstanding debt. The managers know that investors like to receive dividends, and so they are willing to forego some cash to keep their shareholders happy. In fact, some debt is not a bad thing for a company. Most companies have a dividend policy whereby they stipulate what percentage of their cash flow they will pay out. This helps the investor to calculate the dividend yield on a share. For example, if you can calculate that the dividend will be around 10c per share, and the share is currently trading at R1,20, it is easy to work out that the dividend yield is 8,33%. Then you can compare it to what you are receiving from the bank and decide whether it is worth buying the share.

Investors will often buy shares exactly for the dividend yield, but there is no certainty when it comes to dividends. The risk is that the company will not meet your cash flow expectations, will want to use the cash for other things, such as writing down debt or an expansionary programme, and will end up paying out a smaller-than-expected dividend.

Invariably, when a company cuts its dividend, the share price also falls, because all those investors holding the share specifically to receive the dividend will sell the share and buy other higher-yielding shares or put the money into an instrument with a more certain yield. In the case of a company cutting its dividend, it is ideal if the share price rises while you hold the share, so that you make your money on the increase in share price.

Do you remember Webvan? Not many people do. Webvan was an online grocery store founded in 1996 during the dotcom boom. Silicon Valley investors (those smart private equity guys again) such as Sequoia Capital, SoftBank, Goldman Sachs and even Yahoo invested close to $400 million in the company. In November 1999 Webvan listed on the NYSE (share code: WBVN) and raised an additional $375 million by selling just 8% of the company. On the day the Webvan share listed on the stock exchange, it started trading at $15 per share.

> An **INITIAL PUBLIC OFFERING (IPO)** is the occasion when a company issues shares and lists on the stock exchange.

As traders watched the stock through the day, the share price went all the way up to $34 a share. By the end of the day the share had had a little pullback, but still closed 65% higher than where it had started trading – not a bad return for one day. If you're good at maths, you've figured out that by the end of the first trading day, investors had effectively pushed the value of the company to an eye-watering $7,9 billion. A mere five years later this apparently promising company, which had raised money from the Silicon Valley private equity investors, asset managers, traders and ordinary investors, went bankrupt. That's right, the shareholders lost all the money they had used to buy shares in Webvan. Are you wondering what happened to the $375 million the company raised through its IPO? Management spent it!

And this is one of the reasons that shares are considered risky investments. After the bankruptcy Webvan probably sold some of the vans and stock it still owned, but shareholders had no right to that cash. As I have previously explained, that cash had to be distributed pro rata to some of the bondholders. If you were a shareholder to the end, you would have lost all your money. If you were a bondholder, you would have made 5% per annum in interest payments. When the company went bankrupt, there is a chance you might have gotten 10c on the dollar for your initial capital – the money you loaned them.

Going back to our earlier example, if you had been an Apple bondholder you would have made in the region of 1% to 5% per annum. If you were an Apple shareholder, you would have made in the region of 32 400% (no, you didn't read that wrong, that's thirty-two thousand four hundred per cent – or close to 75% per annum).

The choice is easy in hindsight, but is a tough investment decision at the time. This is partly why you need to understand your appetite for risk. Remember this for when I explain the risk/reward continuum. And also remember that shares generally produce higher returns over the medium/long term. But the price you pay for higher returns is volatility; the fact that shares can go through long periods of negative returns. Volatility causes angst and sleepless nights for some people.

Even one of the great economists of all time, John Maynard Keynes, understood that 'the market can stay irrational longer than you can stay solvent'.[10] So, if it's the higher returns you want, brace yourself for a bumpy ride.

Commodities

A commodity is the raw material that is used to create the products that consumers buy every day. Think gold, maize, platinum, oil, silver, cattle, cotton, cocoa, coffee, wood and gas – it's a fairly extensive list.

Commodities trading was originally used as a hedge for the producers and users of the asset – in other words, as a way of protecting themselves from negative movements in the price. Say you are a car manufacturer who needs platinum, which is the main input for making catalytic converters. The price of platinum could fluctuate so much from the start of production to when you need the platinum that you are unable to set a price for your car. What you could do is to buy the platinum at a set price from the producer for delivery when you need it. I don't need to explain that you, as the manufacturer, would want as low a price as possible for the platinum.

On the other side of the spectrum is the producer, who, with his set input costs (plant and machinery, wages for miners, etc) is nervous that the platinum price could drop to below the cost of taking the metal out of the ground. If he could get someone to buy the platinum at a price that makes mining it profitable, he could go ahead and employ miners, set up the drills, and start digging.

In between the two you will find speculators, or traders. Because the timing of buying and delivering the platinum is not perfectly aligned, the speculator will generally trade futures, which is basically a contract between her and the mining company and another contract between her and the car manufacturer. At no stage does the speculator want to take delivery of the platinum, but she does want to make the profit between the buying and selling price.

Commodities have received a bad reputation as being volatile and speculative. However, just as it is a risky strategy to invest in only one company, and less risky to buy a number of shares in different companies, buying and selling a single commodity is perhaps not the best idea. After all, not many of us are savvy enough to be speculators.

At this stage, it is important to understand how the different assets behave. For example, commodities are considered a good hedge against fast-rising inflation. When the rate of inflation is high, it means the demand for goods and services is high. High demand for goods translates into higher demand for the input raw materials (commodities), pushing prices higher. On the other hand, shares and bonds tend to suffer in high-inflation environments.

Commodities are therefore considered to be a good hedge, meaning they bring balance when added to a share and bond portfolio. If you want to hedge out the risk of possible high-inflation environments, where shares and bonds may come under pressure, then commodities are a good way of diversifying. You should look to buy commodity indices rather than single commodities, though.

The one commodity that has always intrigued me is gold. It is a very soft metal, it has few industrial uses, and you cannot eat it. Yet for centuries gold underpinned our monetary system, and it is still considered a 'safe haven' asset. In other words, when it looks like the global economy is under pressure, when shares are plummeting, you will often find gold on the rise.

When gold is on the rise, you could buy shares in gold-mining companies, but be warned that the translation from a higher gold price to a higher gold-mining company share price is not perfect. When it comes to companies, there are many more factors to consider than simply an increasing revenue line (company debt levels, wages, depth and age of the mine and quality of product, to name a few). Analysing gold companies is a very specific skill (often best left to metallurgists turned investment professionals), but for our purposes buying gold ETFs would be a suitable way to gain exposure to gold.

Hedge funds

Perhaps not an asset class on its own, but a type of fund that you need to know about, hedge funds have been around for a long time. They gained prominence in the last couple of decades when individuals such as George Soros, David E Shaw, Ken Griffin, Ray Dalio and the very vocal Bill Ackman hit the headlines for the extraordinary amounts of money they made, not only for themselves, but also for their clients.

> A **HEDGE FUND** differs from a 'normal' fund, in that it is authorised to sell shares it does not own (short selling).

The term 'hedge fund' simply means that if the fund manager thinks the market is going down, but is unsure of timing and magnitude, he can hedge out his risk. Hedge funds employ a number of investment strategies, such as long/short, market neutral and relative value arbitrage, to name a few. For our purposes, hedge funds fall into the category of alternative investments.

One of the best-known hedge funds, and certainly a case study for any student of finance, is Long-Term Capital Management (LTCM), founded by renowned bond trader John Meriwether in 1994. Meriwether surrounded himself with Nobel Prize-winning economists, such as Myron S Scholes and Robert C Merton. In the first second and third years of the fund, LTCM produced returns of 21%, 43% and 41%, respectively (after fees). Then, in 1998, as a result of the Asian financial crisis (1997) and the Russian financial crisis (1998), the fund lost $4,6 billion in less than four months and required a bailout from the US Federal Reserve because of the fund's credit exposure to major banks.

The shock to the financial system caused everyone to sit up and pay attention, and as with every major crisis, regulation was tightened around the institutions that were seen to have caused the crisis. Until recently, hedge fund investments were reserved for qualified investors (QIs), also known as authorised investors. This meant you had to have a net worth of more than $1 million and a decent understanding of the risks associated with hedge funds.

More recently, regulators have been allowing hedge fund managers to offer their funds to retail or unqualified investors under a much stricter regime. Hedge funds were created to generate higher returns when the market turned negative, and with the implementation of stricter regulation, a hedge fund can now offer the retail investor an additional diversification strategy.

Private equity
Very simply, private equity means the shares in a company are not listed on a stock exchange and therefore are not available to the public and have no share code. (As I've mentioned,

we use the words 'equities' and 'shares' interchangeably.) Just as there are fund managers who buy and sell shares in public companies that are listed on a stock exchange, there are fund managers who will buy and sell shares in private companies on your behalf. These private equity funds also fall into the category of alternative investments.

With private equity funds, the fund manager/s decide that a listed company would do better if it was not listed on the stock exchange. Then they buy the listed shares and delist the company, thereby taking it private and turning it into a private equity, unlisted company.

One of the first things you need to be aware of about private equity funds is that, because the shares are not listed, they can be very illiquid. In fact, most private equity funds will require that investors leave their money in the fund for a minimum of five to seven years, with the option to extend the investment term, when they will eventually wind up the fund. Second, the fees in private equity are generally higher than listed shares or bond portfolios.

In private equity funds, managers will charge a 2% annual management fee, based on the assets you have invested with them and 20% of the profits made by the fund. For example, if you invest R1 000 and at the end of the fund's life the profit on the R1 000 invested is R600, the annual fee will be R20 per annum and R120 performance fee.

Private equity funds are mostly reserved for QIs. If you do want to invest in private equity, there are a lot more rules and regulations you need to be aware of; be sure to do your homework before diversifying into this asset class.

Property

Let's look at property as an investment – not as your childhood home, or as a roof over your family's head, but rather as an investment option.

I'm aware of the proliferation, in recent years, of books and theories on how property is the 'only' secure investment to make, or how to become independently wealthy by investing in property, or even how property can be a 'golden visa'. Property has a tangibility and 'safe haven' status that somehow makes it easier to get your head around as an investment option. But let's keep our investment hats on and look at it a bit more clinically.

> **LEVERAGE** is the ability to borrow money to generate a higher return (after paying interest on the loan).

I like property because of its inherent leverage facility. I'm talking about the fact that a bank will lend you money to buy property. If you have only R100 000, there's a good chance the bank will lend you the balance of R900 000 to buy a property worth R1 million.

If you invest R100 000 and make a return of 10% per annum, after five years you've made a profit of R61 051 (it's not R50 000, ie R10 000 per annum, because we assume you've reinvested every year's profit to earn profit on profit. I'll teach you the power of compound interest in Chapter 8, but for now we're focusing on leverage). If you make a return of 10% per annum for the same period on the R1 million, your profit is R610 510. And to think you started with the same R100 000!

This is one of the key selling points of all those books that promise you financial freedom when you invest in property. The dream is premised on the fact that you will earn a rental income as well as benefit from capital appreciation (growth in the value of the property). I'm not going to knock it completely, because, one, I'm no stranger to property investments and, two, there's nothing wrong with sweating your assets and making some money – that's why you're reading this book. However, you should also keep the following in mind:

- *Interest:* If you are going to take out a mortgage to invest in property, don't forget to calculate the interest as an expense (part of your investment). The good news is that you can generally write down this interest charge against tax.

- *Maintenance:* Remember to include the cost of maintenance when you calculate your capital outlay (amount invested). Again, do your homework when it comes to the tax benefits.

- *Time:* Always, always look at your time as part of your investment – you wouldn't work for your employer for free. Maybe you'd do work for yourself at a discounted rate, but when calculating cost of investment, assume that you would have to pay an agent, plumber or electrician to do the work you may be doing. The problem with doing it yourself is that you rarely invoice yourself, and therefore cannot use it as a tax write-down.

The worst thing about leverage is that it works the same on the downside (negative returns/losses) as it does on the upside (profits). If you do not meet your monthly repayment on your mortgage, the bank could repossess your house and you would lose not only the initial R100 000 deposit, but also all the money you have paid in interest, maintenance and labour. Your loss would be 100%.

The same principle applies to any building, be it industrial, commercial, retail (shopping centre) or leisure (hotels, B&Bs and guesthouses), taking into account that specialised buildings need specialised management or agents. If you are buying-to-let, at least remember that if interest rates go up, your mortgage payments increase and your yield (10% per annum in this example) decreases. To give a simple example, if you are charging R10 000 in rent and your mortgage payment is R9 000, your gross profit is R1 000. If interest rates go up and your mortgage repayment goes up in line with it, let's say to R9 250, your profit immediately drops to R750.

Apart from the upside leverage (making more profit by borrowing), another excellent reason to buy property is for diversification in your overall portfolio. Property can be a hedge against inflation and a reliable source of income, once the asset has been paid for. Of course, not everyone can afford to buy a building.

And here's another thing: not everyone wants to deal with agents, plumbers, electricians or tenants. And smart investors don't want to put all their investment eggs into one building, in one suburb of one city in a single province of only one country in the world. Location, location, location – affordability, diversification and yield.

And so we come to the exciting world of listed property. There are numerous listed property funds, which give you exposure to a variety of property types all over the world, in the currency of your choice (and with no conveyancing required by you). For as little as a couple of hundred rands, you can invest in a company that owns and manages some of the best properties across the world.

> **LISTED PROPERTY** consists of funds invested in property assets that are listed on a stock exchange.

The options on listed property funds range from property unit trusts to real estate investment trusts (REITs) and property ETFs. REITs in particular are popular because of the regulation that requires them to pay out 90% of their profits, after costs, to investors. Although the annual yield on a REIT is not defined upfront, like a bond, you will often find a large percentage of REITs in portfolios that are designed for income generation (mostly for investors who are close to retirement). The potential for large swings in the underlying capital valuation of a REIT makes it a less certain instrument than a bond.

> **YIELD** is the annual interest amount you receive expressed in percentage terms. If you are receiving R20 on your R1 000 investment, your yield is 2%. In property terms, yield is simply rent after costs have been deducted (profit).

I mentioned earlier that property is a good hedge against inflation. When there is no inflation, the price of goods does not increase, and that includes property. A landlord will struggle to raise the rent, and the yield on the property will remain unchanged or even decrease, because maintenance is still required as the building ages. It's the same for the factory owner. Without a bit of inflation, he will struggle to increase the price of the goods he is selling. Therefore, revenue will remain the same, which will filter through to the workers on the factory floor because the owner cannot afford to increase wages.

Trust me when I say that some inflation is good. What you do not want is hyperinflation, which we saw in Zimbabwe in the early 2000s. (The South African Reserve Bank has a target inflation rate of between 3% and 6%.) However, if you do have the correct amount of inflation then the landlord, without too much resistance, can increase the rent annually (thereby increasing the yield) and thus the value of the property will increase.

I cannot emphasise strongly enough that property is a good diversifying asset when building your investment portfolio.

Wine and art as asset classes

I spent a couple of years working for a fine wine company in London and San Francisco, and I remember being told that the theory behind investing in wine is to buy at least two cases – one to drink as the years progress, and the other to sell when the wine has reached its peak. When you consider that in 2010 someone paid more than $300 000 for a Methuselah (six litres, equivalent to eight 750 ml bottles) of 1947 Chateau Cheval Blanc, there can be big money in wine.

In theory, the best wines in the world get better with age, as the tannins soften and the flavour improves, but even the best wines peak, and knowing when to drink them is fundamental to wine investing. I do not consider myself a wine investor; but I'm happy to impart the basic knowledge I do have.

There are currently three well-known wine exchanges (almost like stock exchanges, but for wine): London International Vintners Exchange (Liv-ex), Cavex and Berry Bros and Rudd (BBX). Just like the JSE All Share Index, which is an indicator of how well the shares on the JSE are performing, or the Top 40 Index, which is an indicator of how well the top 40 shares by market capitalisation are doing, there is the Liv-ex Fine Wine 1 000 index, which tracks the prices of the top 1000 wines in the world.

Wine and art investors have a name for the origins and history of the asset and how well it has been looked after: it's called 'provenance'. These days, you rarely receive a physical certificate when buying a share or a bond; it's all electronic. When buying property, you will receive the physical property, and the resale value will depend not only on the market, but also how well you've looked after your property. The same goes for wine.

Wine investors rarely take physical home delivery of their wine. It is held in storage in a bonded warehouse, partly to save the investor from paying import duties, and mostly because wine merchants have secure, insured, temperature controlled storage to accommodate their clients.

Not only will you need time for your wine investment to mature (no different from other good investments), but you will also need to get to know the intriguing world of wine investing, starting with the 1855 Bordeaux classifications, which to this day have hardly changed, who the tried and trusted négociants are, what a vertical tasting is, and more importantly, what makes a wine worth buying in a couple of years and where to sell your wines when you are ready to liquidate your portfolio.

While I do not have a creative bone in my body I have often been moved by paintings and statues. Unfortunately, I do not believe that is sufficient to make me a good art investor. For that, there are art dealers, consultants and even wealth managers. Investing in art, particularly contemporary art, is a somewhat specialised area for the investor.

Art has strong investment potential, if you buy well and are prepared to let your investment mature. Some investors enter the art market because they love paintings, sculpture and photography; others are more straightforwardly business-minded. When you look at the media, there are often articles about the high prices paid for this or that painting, while the big global art fairs (Art Basel, Frieze and others) create buzz around the rising stars of contemporary art. As with other asset classes, investing in art often means being in it for the long term.

The art market is fickle and ever-changing, so your choice of art should be based on your own taste as much as on its investment value. Spend time in commercial galleries, talk to dealers and auctioneers, and build up your knowledge about artists whose work you admire before you consider investing. There are experts who can assist investors who would like to add fine art to their investment portfolio. Financial services giant Sanlam, for instance, offers, a specialised art advisory service.

There is no lack of information on the returns that can be generated from investing in art. According to the 2018 Global

Art Market Report by ArtPrice.com,[11] which covered only the first six months of the year, global auction turnover on fine art (painting, sculpture, drawing, photography, prints, installation) rose 18%, to a total of $8,45 billion. Of 262 000 lots sold, the USA posted a total turnover of $3,3 billion, while sales in China amounted to $2 billion. In the UK, auction turnover was up 18% to $1,9 billion, and growth in European markets was strong. Modern art (work produced from the 1860s to the 1970s) remains the mainstay of the high-end market, accounting for 46% of total turnover. Sales of works by Modigliani and Picasso both generated results above the $100 million threshold. However, the global price index for contemporary art rose by 27%, rivalling the S&P 500 index.

Needless to say, it's that last point that caught my interest. In a year when the S&P 500 index returned a measly 3% (including reinvested dividends) in the first half, the contemporary art global price index rose by 27%.

Impact investing

Impact investing can include investments in a company (listed or unlisted), property, another impact fund and agricultural or developmental land. It falls somewhere between an asset class and an investment product because the tangible underlying it is not a class of its own. What makes impact investing different from the other investments is that the measure of success is not simply financial return, but rather measurable social and environmental impacts.

It is important to focus on the word 'measurable' because it refers to tangible changes effected by your investment. For instance, how many jobs were created by investing in the company? How was the environment positively impacted by the investment in the company or the purchase of the land? How many lives were positively impacted in the village into which the company expanded?

Impact investing is not philanthropy or corporate socially responsible investing (CSRI). Investors in an impact fund are looking for not only return of capital, but also a tangible (financial and beneficial socio-economic) return on capital. Similarly, impact investing is not environmental, social and governance (ESG) investing, which seeks to avoid companies that do bad things like polluting rivers, chopping down rain forests, displacing communities, etc. This is a phenomenon we call 'negative screening', whereas impact investing is about positive screening, or going out with the intent to find investments that will make a positive impact.

You might be wondering why not all investment funds are impact funds (if you're going to manage my money, then invest it in doing good in the world), or why not all investors insist on being invested in impact funds. Primarily it's because the prospect of higher returns outweighs the need to mitigate environmental damage. Think of companies that create oil spills, or that make products from palm oil, or that fail to rehabilitate worked-out mines: the list is endless but the profits are extraordinary.

It is widely believed that impact funds produce lower financial returns for the investor. On the surface, it would appear that more resources (human capital and time) are required to manage an impact fund, because screening for and monitoring investments is a time-consuming process that is additional to the normal financial analysis required. Therefore, the returns are lower. In addition, most impact investing is still private equity, and carries with it all the risks of private equity, such as illiquidity, uncertainty and volatility of returns.

Cryptocurrency

I will discuss cryptocurrency briefly, not because I believe it is an asset class, but because I know many people are curious about it. Some may even consider it an asset class.

On 18 August 2018, the world's first cryptocurrency turned ten years old (as measured from the registration date of the bitcoin.org domain name). The true identity of Satoshi Nakamoto remains a mystery, and even more intriguing is his apparent disappearance and handover of the key code in 2010, but it is widely accepted that he is the founder of the electronic currency.

Today, Bitcoin is seen as a way of liberating us from the shackles of the banking and tax system, but we would do well to remember that the first major users of Bitcoin were Silk Road transactors on the so-called dark web. By the time Bitcoin was a decade old, there were already 3 000 other cryptocurrencies, including something called CryptoKitty on the Ethereum blockchain.

In my opinion, the real innovation and value for investors lies in the blockchain. Fundamentally, the blockchain is the digital ledger on which the electronic currencies are recorded. Investing in blockchain would be an investment in the future. Like deciding which share to invest in, if you wanted to invest in the blockchain, I would recommend researching providers with as critical an eye as you would do any listed company.

With over 200 exchanges trading in cryptocurrencies, it's hard to say which cryptocurrency will survive and thrive. In 2017, when Bitcoin became 'popular', the price rose over 1 000% to reach a peak of $19 666 per coin from $998 at the beginning of that year. This is spectacular when you consider that the first transactions in Bitcoin were done at $0,30 in 2011. But by April 2019, the price had fallen back to around $5 000 per coin.

Where to from here? Well, that's anyone's guess. I feel strongly that the coin itself has no underlying tangible value – its value is based on supply and demand, and a healthy dose of marketing.

Proponents of cryptocurrency hate it when I liken the phenomenon to the Dutch tulip bulb craze of the 1630s – considered to be the first speculative bubble. During the height of the craze, a single tulip bulb could fetch as much as six times the average Dutchman's wage, with some bulbs changing hands as many as ten times a day. Everyone wanted to own tulip bulbs. Suddenly, in February 1637, buyers refused to pay the extraordinarily high prices and stopped pitching up for what had become the regular auctions of the bulbs. The bubble had burst. And, suffice to say, a tulip bulb now costs less than a glass of wine.

You do not have to be invested in every single one of the above-mentioned asset classes, but it is important to know that the different asset classes behave differently, and you can make use of this knowledge to build a diversified portfolio that will reduce your risk.

Investment products

Investment products are a combination of asset classes or shares to make investing easier. Investment products include RAs (discussed in Chapter 3), ETFs, unit trusts and tax-free savings accounts (TFSAs). Each of the asset classes described above comes with specific risks, optimal investment periods and expected returns. In addition, it is not always easy to invest small amounts of money into some of the asset classes or subcategories.

You may decide you like the risk/return profile of retail property in South Africa, but you have limited funds and cannot buy an entire shopping centre. To resolve this issue, there are funds that aggregate investors' money and invest in the big-ticket items. In this asset class, property funds can be listed or unlisted.

Unit trusts, also known as collective investment schemes and, in some countries, mutual funds, are a very popular investment product. With unit trusts, an administrator will gather many people's money and pool it in a fund for the asset manager to allocate to assets (in other words, to invest). Because each investor will invest different amounts of money, and at different times in the life of the fund, the administrator will unitise the fund and value the units on a daily basis, so that when investor B, C, D . . . starts investing, they will purchase a unit at the price registered on that particular day.

Below is a practical example.

A fund manager starts a tech dollar fund and buys:

10 shares each of Amazon (share code: AMZN) at $1 500 per share ($15 000)

10 shares of Facebook (FB) at $150 per share ($1 500)
80 shares of Tencent (TCEHY)[12] at $35 per share ($2 800)
17 shares of Microsoft (MSFT) at $100 per share ($1 700)
Total portfolio value: $21 000

Day one: Investor A invests $21 000.
Day two: Each share price increases by 5% and the port-
folio is valued at $21 050.
Day three: Share prices increase again and the portfolio
is worth $21 100.
Investor B has $21 000 and wants to buy into the fund.

However, even though both invested the same amount of
money, it would be unfair to Investor A if they both owned
50% of the portfolio and his $21 100 was suddenly 50% of
$41 100, i.e. $20 550. Where did the other $550 profit disap-
pear to? What the administrator has to do is issue units at
initialisation of the fund:

Day one: The fund issues 1 000 units at $21 each.
Day three: Each unit is worth $21,10.
Investor B invests $21 000 and gets 995,2607 units ($21 000
divided by $21,10).
Total portfolio value: $42 100 (total units 1995,2607)
Investor A portfolio valuation: $21 100 (1 000 units)
Investor B portfolio valuation: $21 000 (995,2607)

A week later the portfolio value has increased by 10% to
$46 310 (total units 1995,2607 at $23,201).
Investor A portfolio valuation: 1 000 units at $23,201
per unit = $23,210

Investor B portfolio valuation: 995 2607 units at $23,201 per unit = $23,091

What if Investor C doesn't have $21 000 to invest, but only $232? No problem, she can buy 10 units. Each investor will benefit from the same access to an expert fund manager, the same asset class and the same return profile.

Unit trusts can invest in a variety of assets, from shares, to bonds, property, commodities or a combination of assets, and even in other funds. The list is not infinite, but it can be overwhelming.

Tax-free savings accounts (TFSAs)

A recent addition to the investment landscape in South Africa has been the tax-free savings account. In order to increase the very low rate of saving in South Africa, in 2015 the government introduced TFSAs, which allow the investor to save or invest up to R33 000 (the limit was increased from R30 000 in 2018) per annum, with a maximum lifetime limit of R500 000, without paying tax on interest, dividends and capital gains.

I've specifically referred to savings and investments for your TFSA because you can choose simply to save in this vehicle (money market or fixed deposit) or you can invest (shares, bonds, etc). As you now know, each of these carries their own risk/return profile, and the choice will depend on your age and appetite for risk. The usefulness of this vehicle lies in the fact that the first portion of your investment can be tax-free.

KEY POINTS

1. Different types of assets behave differently in specific economic environments.

2. You can combine the different asset classes to design a portfolio that suits your particular needs.

3. You can utilise the different asset classes to manage the risk in your portfolio.

6

Who's who in the investment zoo

Mention the word 'investments' and most people's eyes glaze over. If you advise them to see a financial advisor, you might as well have told them to pay a visit to the finance minister to discuss their household budget. But investing shouldn't be that intimidating, which is why I wrote this book.

To see that finance, budgeting and investing is well within your grasp, you need to understand that the financial advisor is there to assist you. Many people see finance and banking as one big machine, but just as there are pharmacists, nurses, general practitioners, dentists, physiotherapists, nutritionists and psychologists to take care of your health, so too are there financial advisors, asset managers, traders and banks to support your financial health.

I've outlined the main ones for you in this chapter, using a zoological theme to give you a sense of where they all belong.

Banks *(tortoises)*
Banks started out as money lenders when merchants needed to purchase ships and hire crew to transport goods around the world. Banks loaned merchants the money, trusting that they

would be repaid on the merchant's return. The means of transport, merchandise and what people get paid to do may have changed, but, in essence, the banking system remains the same.

Today, the banking system is considered the heart of the economy. The trust on which the system is built is all-pervasive. When it comes to financial services, banks can be likened to the tortoise in Aesop's fable of the tortoise and the hare. Banks tend to be slow to innovate and are all-encompassing in that they offer a large range of products (transactional banking, lending, asset management, trading platforms, research and even airport lounge access), and they have outlasted almost every other financial services business.

In core banking, you give the bank your money, trusting that they will give it back to you when you need it, and they lend you money, almost trusting that you will give it back to them when you are supposed to. I say 'almost', because mostly the bank will expect an asset as collateral against the loan, and if you do not repay them, they will collect the asset and sell it in order to get their money back.

The bank takes your money, pays you interest – for example, 5% – and lends that same money to someone else at a higher rate, for example 8%. That's really how banks make their money. The banking regulators insist on the bank's holding a certain amount of money in liquid, easily accessible form to be able to cover withdrawals.

And this is why we say banking is built on trust, because we do not expect everyone to withdraw all their money at once. This trust is so deeply entrenched in the system that not many people consider their bank deposits to be a risky investment. If we all withdrew our money at once, the bank would be forced to call in the loans they had made. And if you couldn't repay your loan, they would have to insist on taking the house or car you'd bought with the mortgage or car loan they gave you. Unfortunately, not many people have more savings than they have debt.

Imagine if everyone lost faith in a bank and started withdrawing their money. This is called a 'run on the bank'. That bank would have to dissolve, and not everyone would be able to get their money out – not only individuals, but also other banks (because banks borrow from each other). This would be disastrous for any economy. During the global financial crisis of 2008–2009, many banks were bailed out by governments to avoid economic disaster. As recently as 2017, the oldest bank in the world, Banca Monte dei Paschi di Siena, which was established in 1472 and traces its roots to a Roman Catholic charitable institution established to lend money to the poor, had to be bailed out by the Italian government.

Core banking services include transaction accounts (to pay and receive money) and financing for individuals, companies and projects (lending). The role of banks in the investment world has become fairly prominent because they now also offer advisory services, trading accounts and investment advice. More people have a need for the core banking services than the individual investment services, but you can see how a bank with a large client base would want to capture more of their client business by offering additional services such as investments and insurance.

Banks may not have been the first to offer investment services, and they are certainly not the biggest in the investment world, but they can almost hand-pick the wealthiest clients for their investment offerings. Have you ever noticed how banks classify prestigious clients and offer them as many services as possible to ensure those clients keep all their business with the one bank? You didn't really think your bank's giving you free airport lounge access because they thought you deserved it, did you? Obviously not. The guy behind the counter at the NÜ health food café the other day reminded me about it when I ordered a smoothie and said, 'Hang on, I have a free smoothie from Discovery.'

He smiled wryly and said, 'It's not really free.'

On the subject of Discovery, I'm looking forward to becoming a banking client of theirs, after decades of being with my 'old' bank. Not for the free smoothies, but because they have promised to contribute up to an additional 20% to my RA investment (T&C's apply!). An insurance company moving into the world of banking, and offering me investment services – now that I can't resist.

Financial advisors/planners (giraffes)

Giraffes are the ladies and gentlemen you are most likely to encounter on your road to financial freedom. Their job is to assist people like you, to help you make sense of your financial situation and the products on offer, to help you design a plan that best suits your financial goals, to revise that plan as needed, and, finally, to ensure that you get through retirement comfortably.

They should all have done their exams and must be registered with the relevant regulatory institutions. Like giraffes, financial advisors tend to have an air of elegance and eloquence about them; they are usually well-dressed and charming (of course, apart from acting in an advisory role, they are also in sales and need to be presentable to you, the client).

Giraffes sell their time. They spend hours meeting with clients and doing specific client financial analysis, as well as researching available investment products, comparing prices and returns, and assessing their suitability to their clients' financial goals.

Financial advisors generally do not charge an upfront fee; they get commission based on the products they advise their clients to purchase. They may have to spend the same amount of time with a client who has just started working, has little investment capital, and needs the basic products as with a client who has amassed millions of rands and needs an investment plan.

You can clearly see where most of the giraffes' commission will come from – they feed from the highest branches. However, if a giraffe is smart, he will build up a decent client base and help his clients grow their capital, leading to higher commission and a good reputation as his clients grow with his career.

Asset managers (pachyderms)

The pachyderms are known mostly by their herd name, such as Coronation, Old Mutual, Melville Douglas, Investec and Allan Gray, or they are often associated with big banks such as Nedbank, Standard Bank, UBS, Pictet, Julius Bäer, Credit Suisse and Morgan Stanley, to name a few. I've called them 'pachyderms', a category that can be subdivided into elephants, rhinos and hippos.

At the head of the herd is the Oracle of Omaha, Warren Buffett, and his long-time friend and business partner, Charlie Munger, who manage investments in their listed investment company, Berkshire Hathaway, which as of financial year-end 2018 held assets to the value of $707 billion.

I'm not sure if Warren Buffett is revered more for how much money he has made over his years of investing or for the fact that he still lives in the same house and neighbourhood he did in the years before he became one of the world's most successful investors and a multibillionaire. Or maybe it's because one of his biggest treats is to buy himself an Egg McMuffin at McDonald's when he's feeling 'rich'.

Buffett's net worth in 2019 was recorded to be $82,5 billion, which he started accumulating in his teens when he first got interested in investing. Many professionals have tried to emulate Buffett's style of investing, some successfully and others not so much. Bear in mind that Buffett is known not only for being smart, but also for living a frugal lifestyle, and in 2006 pledged to donate 99 % of his wealth to charity.

My triathlon training partner and I share a lot of memes to keep ourselves motivated to spend hours swimming, cycling and running, and Buffett's story reminds me of one we recently shared: 'To succeed, make sure you're not just motivated by the end goal, but you're so passionate about the process that you'll love the journey and stay on track.'

In my mind, this completely sums up the phenomenon that is Warren Buffett. No doubt he loves making money, but more importantly, he loves reading his newspaper, analysing companies, and making investment decisions.

Asset managers, such as State Street in the US, have the

potential to grow to an astonishing size. State Street manages $2,8 trillion in assets and in 2017 generated revenue in excess of $11 billion. The company offers a range of investment products and work closely with the other animals in the park to deliver their products to the market.

The largest South African asset manager is Coronation, which as at their financial year-end 2018 managed R505 billion. An asset manager can offer you anything from an emerging-market-focused fund to an equity fund, impact investment or (ESG) bond fund.

Each herd is made up of individual asset managers. They are sure-footed, move slowly, assimilate huge amounts of information, and are responsible for making the decisions on which shares, bonds, derivatives, property or unlisted stocks are bought and sold in the markets of their choosing.

A pachyderm is wholly focused on finding assets that meet her investment criteria and will buy or sell these assets based on the projected risk and return expectations. The reputations of pachyderms are based on how well they deliver returns to their clients; hence the fame of one such as Warren Buffett, whose fund has returned close to 750 000% since 1964.

Fund managers are generally specialists in a particular asset class, whether it is shares in a company (equities), debt (bonds), derivatives and developed or emerging markets. Elephants such as Mark Mobius, Bill Gross and Paul Tudor Jones have led their herds for decades with unwavering discipline, but may not necessarily have become household names. Every day of their lives is spent reading, analysing and investing large amounts of money for their clients. Each of these well-known fund managers has left their mark on the investment world in some way. Mark Modius has become the go-to expert in the area of emerging markets, and is known for writing policy and as a sought-after guest speaker. Paul Tudor Jones became famous for predicting the Black Monday stock market crash (October 1987) and tripling his investment. He has also seeded a number of new up-and-coming hedge fund managers and founded the Robin Hood Foundation – a charity capitalised by other fund managers.

Elephants (long-only equity managers)

The majority of invested capital remains in the hands of what we call 'long-only equity managers'. These managers are a subset of the larger fund manager group. The term 'fund manager' can mean a professional who manages a bond fund, an equity fund, a property fund, a private equity fund, etc. Some managers, whether equity or bond managers, can also be hedge fund managers (we'll get to that later), but the long-only equity manager is someone who primarily manages large amounts of equity (share) portfolios.

The Disney animated film *The Jungle Book* is a beloved classic, and almost everyone can name Mowgli's friends and enemies, such as Baloo, King Louie and Shere Khan. However, not everyone can recall Colonel Hathi. You may remember him for his strict military drills, demands for obedience and dignified storytelling of 'How Fear Came'. Long-only equity managers are the Colonel Hathis of this world.

Fund managers spend their days analysing companies. They build spreadsheets with all the relevant financial data, they look carefully at the sector each company belongs to, formulate a view of the countries, economies and regulatory environments these companies find themselves operating under, meet with management to probe for insights into future plans and prospects of the company, and then decide if it is worth owning shares in the company. If the answer is a yes, the traditional fund manager (as they are still called in some circles) will add the share to his portfolio.

Once the share reaches full potential (or is fully priced) the fund manager may decide to sell the shares. This is where having a thick skin is crucial, because even though elephants spend many hours researching and years getting to know companies and the people that run them, shares do not move up in a straight trajectory. There is always an unexpected slowdown in the economy, a surprise disappointing result or piece of legislation that weighs on the share, or, as in the case of electric-car manufacturer Tesla in mid-2018, an erratic CEO.

It was at this time that Elon Musk, who we knew was a bit gung-ho to start with, suddenly started tweeting about how he was planning to take his company private at a price well above where the share was trading ($420 versus the last traded $369), and that he had secured the financial backing to effect the change. His comments could have been construed as market manipulation, which is illegal under US securities law. Musk later explained that a combination of overwork and lack of sleep had led him to speak rashly. Now, no analyst or investor wants to hear a CEO say he can't cope. But, a couple of weeks later, after two senior directors resigned and Musk was caught on camera smoking weed, the Tesla share price plummeted to $263: a mighty fall from the lofty promises of world domination. If you were the fund manager holding that share, what would you do? Hold on? Cut your losses and run? Because there was a reason you bought the share in the first place, you would have to ask whether the fundamentals of the company had changed, or whether Musk's behaviour represented a mere blip on the share price's meteoric rise from $17 in 2010.

Since some of you will want to invest in shares, let's try to understand the mind of an elephant by looking at a specific example. The price of oil has come down and the minimum driving age has been reduced, and now you're considering how to take advantage of this situation. Start by zooming out and looking at the possible sectors that could benefit from these fundamental changes. These are the questions many elephants would try to find answers to:

- Do you invest in a platinum producer? Consider that the main use of platinum is in making catalytic converters used in petrol-driven cars.
- Or, do you decide to invest in a company that produces electric cars?
- Is the future of environmentally friendly cars near enough the tipping point – the point at which they become so widely used that they replace petrol-driven cars – or do we wait another five to ten years before electric cars become commonplace and sales really start to soar?

There isn't a fund manager alive who has a crystal ball, but the answers to these questions will be based on the fund manager's informed opinion. If the fund manager decides that electric cars are the future, and she believes that sales of these cars are going to rise over the next two years, then it's time to start looking at the fundamentals of companies that produce electric cars.

Rhinoceroses (bond managers)

Bond managers, or rhinoceroses, have a fabulously nerdy orientation[13] and a horn that says, 'I'm numeric and on point'. The rhino spends his days reviewing economic situations, looking at spreadsheets, and deciding if a bond is cheap or expensive.

Bonds tend to be mean-reverting instruments, meaning that they quickly tend to their average price or yield, and therefore bond managers look for cheap or expensive prices, or, better yet, yields that match their required return expectations. The greatest risk associated with bonds is the risk of default, that is, of the issuer not being able to repay the nominal value of the bond at its maturity, or to meet interest payments during the life of the bond. Therefore, like the equity fund manager, the bond manager must understand the company or government that is issuing the bond, as well as the cash flow of the issuer.

We've often heard talk of rating agencies such as Moody's, Fitch Ratings and Standard & Poor's. Bond managers tend to rely on the agencies to do a lot of the deciding on whether a government or company is creditworthy, and what the risk level associated with each of these is. Credit rating is a global system we've all bought into, but as the global financial crisis of 2008–2009 proved, it is by no means foolproof. Credit rating agencies have been criticised for having been behind the curve and not foreseeing the crisis.

Hippopotamuses (hedge fund managers)

Another subset of the pachyderms are the hippopotamuses, because they are as comfortable living on land as they are in the water. Like traditional fund managers, the job of the hedge fund manager is to go in search of assets with appropriate risk return characteristics, and then buy or sell accordingly. The crucial difference is that a hippopotamus (aka hedgehog or 'hedgie') can sell shares or bonds she does not own . . . and this is where it gets 'curiouser and curiouser'.

When it comes to investing, people mostly think about buying shares. In the investment trade, this is called 'going long' (remember the long-only fund manager?). Investors will sell the shares they own only when they think the shares will no longer increase in value, or when they need liquidity.

Hedge fund managers definitely do that, but they are also authorised to sell shares or indices they do not own. This is called 'going short'. Clearly, shares not only move up, but also move down, and as much as there is money to be made when a share increases in value, there is also potential profit to be made if you sell the shares at a certain price and buy them back when the share price has fallen.

In order to sell shares they do not own, hedge fund managers need to borrow the shares. Their prime broker, basically a bank or financial institution, will source the shares – in other words, find someone who is a long-term owner of the shares and is willing to lend them (at a fee, of course) to the short seller. The fee is usually between 0,2% and 5%, depending on how much demand there is to borrow the share.

Once the hedge fund manager has sold the shares or index, she watches in anticipation to see if the share or index will fall in price, at which point she will buy it back at a lower price than she had sold it for, in order to make a profit.

When a hedge fund manager shorts shares or indices, she is considered to be hedging her portfolio, that is, reducing the risk of a possible downturn. When the market turns, the loss incurred will be offset by the profit she makes on the shares she shorted.

As an example, let's say a hedge fund manager thinks that Woolworths will report outstanding results from its offshore operations in its upcoming year-end financial report. However, the local economy is generally in a bad state and the hedgie thinks this could negatively affect all retail shares on the JSE, but she is not sure about the timing of this negative news. She may go 'long' by buying Woolworths shares, and hedge out (reduce) any risk from potential disappointing local macroeconomic news. In so doing, the hedgie will make money when the Woolworths share increases in value, and when the rest of her portfolio decreases in value. The trick is to make more money on one side of the trade than on the other.

Let's say that the hedgie has gone long (bought) an equal amount of R1 million in Woolworths shares and is going short R1 million of the retail index. If the Woolworths shares increase by 10% she will make R100 000 (excluding costs). If the index rises by 5%, she will lose R50 000 (excluding costs), thereby making a net profit of R50 000.

Why bother going short the index and not just take the full R100 000? Because no investor can see into the future, and there are unforeseen circumstances that the fund manager is hedging herself against.

This trade also works in reverse, as long as the quantum of increases and decreases is in her favour. If the index falls by 10% and the Woolworths shares fall by 5%, she will also make R50 000 to R100 000 in profit from shorting the index, and a R50 000 loss from being long the Woolworths shares.

When it doesn't work is when Woolworths shares perform worse than the index, that is, when the index is up 10% and the Woolworths shares are up only 5%. This is why the hedge fund manager has to understand the overall market and have conviction about the movements of share prices, risk and her quantum of hedging.

In some instances, ordinary investors are also allowed to do this, but I would warn against it because of simple mathematics. If you buy a share for R100, your upside potential is unlimited – the share can double, quadruple, increase a hundredfold and still continue increasing. In these instances, you will make R100, R300 or even R9 900 and more in profit (excluding costs). If the share falls to zero, your loss is limited to R100.

Now, if you short that same share, and it falls to zero, you will make a profit of R100. If, however, the share doubles, quadruples or even increases a hundredfold without your having closed out your position, you will lose R100, R300 or R9 900 or more because you have not bought back the shares and returned them to the lender, and because the share can increase exponentially, your potential losses are unlimited. Not a pretty picture.

So, why short shares? Simply, because it can serve as a good hedge, and because even though the stock market trends higher over the long term, it never moves up in a straight line.

'Hippopotamus' seems an unfortunate nickname for such an agile group of investors, but when you consider that in 2016 the top ten US hedge fund managers made $11 billion, you can understand why they are considered one of the largest players in the investment zoo. Furthermore, thanks to them, '2 and 20' is not an uncommon phrase in the world of investing. It refers to the fees hedge fund managers charge their clients – 2% management fee per annum – while taking 20% of the profits. That's big.

Hedgies are also known for being some of the smartest investors around. Generally, they do not like the limelight, and some of them believe that investing in secret gives them the edge. For the most part, they think being feared is cool. Steve Cohen, a well-known hedge fund manager and founder of SAC Capital, has been known to attempt to buy the rights to all photographs of himself so as to limit publicity. It has been said of Bill Ackman, founder of Pershing, that the only thing bigger than his fund is his ego. In 2015 he managed close to $20 billion. Ackman is famous for shorting Herbalife, calling it a pyramid scheme and waiting for the share to fall to zero. However, his self-confidence and $1 billion investment was ill-placed when the share he sold at $45 traded up to $92 in the first year as he slowly built up his position. You can see that if he thought it was a good trade to sell at $45, when the share price went up to $60 it would be an even better trade as the share had further to fall to zero and he could have made even more money. Surely, then, when the share price increased to $80 there was even more money to be made when it eventually fell to zero? There's a fine line between holding your ground when the stock market moves against you (believing that it is a short-term move) and reviewing your position as things change.

But not all hedge fund managers are weird or to be feared. One of my favourites is Ray Dalio, the founder of Bridgewater Associates. Dalio tripled his first investment of $300, which he made at the tender age of 12, and by April 2018 he had a net worth of $17.4 billion. He is known as a generous philanthropist and is proof that not all hedgies deserve their grumpy reputation.

Big cats (traders)

I've worked with enough traders, or big cats, to know that some of them literally growl, hiss and roar. They very rarely purr. More than once, I have been on the receiving end of a roar when I unwittingly got between the predator and his prey. Big cats come in the form of panthers, tigers, leopards and even lions. They're born hunters: stealthy, fast and with a laser focus when in search of their prey.

Traders stand in the pit or sit in front of their computers, day in, day out, looking at the numbers on multiple screens, mostly waiting to take advantage of mispricing and turn a quick profit. There is the executing trader, who acts on instruction from his clients – 'Buy 1 000 Tesla shares at the average price of the day'. In this case, it is the trader's job to understand how the Tesla shares trade, to watch the newswires for any headlines that may affect the share price and to deliver to his client the best price possible.

The proprietary trader trades for her 'own book'. She buys and sells shares, holding them for days or weeks in order to maximise profit.

Electronic trading has exponentially increased the pace at which trades are processed. Imagine the pressure on the traders when price discovery happens faster than they can blink because of the combination of the nature of news and the rate of flow of information in the modern age, and the speed at which one can execute large trades. Remember I mentioned the National Stock Exchange of India, which claims to have 'attained nirvana' by processing trades at the speed of light? I know some mathematical geniuses and analysts who know companies inside out, but none of them can do calculations at the speed of light. The world does not stand still, and before we knew it we had electronic trading. Some may say this will eliminate the human trader, but there are benefits and nuances to having a human hand on the enter key. Artificial intelligence and computer programming have come a long way, but it is still very difficult to upload past experience and emotional quotient.

As a medium- or long-term investor, I believe we need to shut out the 'noise' of daily or even weekly share movements. Bearing this in mind also helps calm your nerves when you see the value of your portfolio moving down; the movement might be due to structural economic changes that last a couple of years, or it might just be short-term market 'noise'.

The zookeepers (platforms)

The average non-professional investor does not have access to the stock market. Stockbroking licences can be obtained from the regulator – in South Africa, this is the Financial Sector Conduct Authority (FSCA) – and come with an enormous amount of regulation and capital requirements.

To buy or sell shares, the investor needs to go through a trading or investment platform. Even professional traders go through platforms, which allow them to enter trades on the stock exchange. So, you could talk directly to an individual or you could trade electronically on a trading platform such as EasyEquities.

There are also platforms where investors can access funds managed by the various professional fund managers (unit trusts, long only, offshore, fixed income, equities, hedge funds, etc). I work closely with the team at Wealthport, who offer cost-effective investments, including TFSAs, RAs and discretionary investments.

Whales (the pachyderm of the sea)

The industry uses the term 'whales' as a catch-all for anyone who manages or trades in such large quantities that it's almost impossible to comprehend. Whales can be long-only or hedge fund managers, cryptocurrency traders or bond traders. In short, a whale is anyone who has enough capital clout that they stand out and, generally, are able to 'move the market' – impact the price of a share – through their trades. As you become more involved in your investment portfolio, it is worth knowing that whales exist because of the impact they have on share portfolios when they express their view through trading.

In recent history, whales have become synonymous with Bitcoin traders and owners. Despite the hype about Bitcoin, it is still a relatively small market, with only 21 million Bitcoin in existence. It is estimated (because I don't think anyone knows for sure) that 40% of the market is owned by

1 000 Bitcoin whales. Even in a depressed market where the cryptocurrency is trading at $5 000 per coin, that's $42 billion between 1 000 people. So you can see how, if one of these Bitcoin traders decided it was time to sell, they could, with relative ease, manipulate the price of the currency.

My analogy for whales is also interchangeable with the term BSD (Big Swinging Dick),[14] made famous by author Michael Lewis in his 1989 bestseller *Liar's Poker*.

Lemmings

This refers to anyone who follows a herd mentality. If you see a big sell-off in the market, are you likely to sell your shares as well? I believe that this happens mostly because people are not confident in their own decisions to own shares, and when they see the market falling, they think they've made a mistake and therefore follow those they think are better informed. They may well be right sometimes, but there are times when a contrarian view is useful.

Crazy things market participants say

When you want to start trading on the stock market, it might be useful to know a few terms that are often used, some of which are rather strange.

- *Stagflation:* A scenario in which a country has a high rate of inflation, low economic growth and high unemployment.
- *Buy and hold:* This strategy refers to the idea that an investor will buy shares with a plan to hold them for an indefinite period, so that they will forget about the shares and not review the shareholding.

- *Taking profits:* Simply getting out of your shares when you've made money on the trade.

- *Stop losses:* The opposite of taking profits. This is an order to sell a share when it has fallen to a certain level, thereby putting a cap on the potential loss.

- *Black box trading:* Trading strategies based on complicated algorithms and executed by high-speed computers.

- *Flash crash:* This is a sharp downward move in the market of between 5% and 10%, usually attributed to automated trading such as black box or algorithmic trading.

- *Bull market* and *bear market:* A bull market refers to a consistently rising market on the back of positive sentiment, while a bear market refers to a market where asset prices are falling. Just as in life there are optimists and pessimists, so are there market participants who are either bullish or bearish (positive or negative) and therefore they are called 'bulls' or 'bears'. The saying, 'Bulls and bears, who cares?', is most appropriate to the long-term investor. We know the market will go through cycles, and we can't predict or time the rise or fall of the market, so who cares?

- *Doves* and *hawks:* The terms 'bulls' and 'bears' are used in relation to shares, but can also be used across a range of asset classes. In the world of interest rates, the complementary comparison is 'doves' and 'hawks'. Doves are people who think that lower interest rates are needed at any time, while hawks want higher interest rates.

- *Bear trap:* Directly related to the negative sentiment of a bear market, a bear trap is when a share price declines after a healthy rise, and traders and investors think this is the sign of the share falling further. However, then the opposite happens and the share rises, causing all the short sellers to reverse their position or risk losing more money. This in turn causes a sharper rise in the share price, and you'll often find that when the short-covering ends, the share price stays relatively flat or falls again. The irony is only emphasised. A bull trap is the reverse of a bear trap, but is not used as often.

The world of investing also has its share of funny expressions that market participants use regularly:

Dead cat bounce

So many people find this one the funniest of the lot, because of the graphic image it evokes. When the stock market has a little rise after a big drop in value, but then resumes its downward trajectory, the little bounce is often referred to as a 'dead cat bounce'. Think about a share that has really bad fundamentals, or reports a horrible set of results at its biannual results presentation. Investors are more likely to want to get rid of any stock they own, and short sellers will sell the share in the hope that they will make a profit as the news reaches the market and the bad fundamentals play out in the share price. However, as the share falls, some investors may think it has fallen sufficiently to reflect some value, or the short sellers have made enough money and are buying back their positions. This will cause the share to rise, but could well cause a dead cat bounce if the rest of the market thinks the share is still overvalued and then continue to sell the share lower.

Bottom fishing

This expression refers to investors and traders who buy up shares after the market has had a protracted sell-off. They're buying shares in the hope that this is the bottom of the downward trend, and that from here the shares will bounce upward. It is particularly apt for the asset manager who sees value in a share but is reticent to buy it because he thinks there is still some downside, even though he is confident the realistic share value is much higher than where it is currently trading. For him, the risk is that the share won't actually decline further and he will miss out on the lower price (and subsequent higher profit). A variant of this scenario is 'Only monkeys pick bottoms'.

Catch a falling knife

When a share falls dramatically but traders think the reaction was overdone and they still see value in the share and therefore want to buy it, you'll often hear them say, 'Don't catch a falling knife'. This means that the share could fall further and that you should wait a while longer. This is the more vivid cousin of bottom fishing. If you're a short-term trader, being able to understand what motivates other buyers and sellers in the stock market is a helpful skill to acquire; it's more intuitive than scientific, but a skill nonetheless.

No one ever went broke booking a profit

This means that when a stock price increases and you've made a tidy little profit, you should sell the share. However, there are those who want to make more profit and then hang on to the share even when the downside risk is higher than the upside possibility. Then you need to tell them it is probably better to sell the share and take the profit, because 'No one ever went broke booking a profit'.

Sell in May and go away

This expression is based on the theory that the summer months in the northern hemisphere produce lower or negative returns than the rest of the year. The recommendation is that investors and traders sell their shares in May and move the money into a safe money market account, and then come back for the 'Halloween Indicator' (31 October) and buy shares. Could it be that traders sell their positions before they go on holiday? Absolutely. Research shows this is in fact true for a large part of history. Traders don't want to spend their holiday worrying that a market influencer will make a statement that could negatively impact the shares in their fund. This has become such a phenomenon that you have to ask whether traders sell because they are afraid the market will turn negative, or does the market turn negative because traders are selling? The jury is still out. Cause or effect?

Only when the tide goes out can you see who's been swimming without shorts

This saying has been attributed to Warren Buffett, and the imagery still makes me smile. It is the counter to 'A rising tide lifts all boats'. Whether you are a good stock picker or a bad stock picker, chances are that when the overall market goes up, your shares will increase in value along with the market – unless you've chosen complete duds – and so every investor or trader looks like a star. However, when things get tough, highly indebted companies, and those with lower margins, inferior products and bad management, are the ones that suffer the most. In a negative market, illiquid shares tend to fall faster than the liquid shares, and from an investment portfolio point of view, these are the shares that will have the more negative impact. As an investor, you should identify these struggling companies and avoid them.

I hope that knowing the different players in the world of finance and investments will help you to find a starting point and make everything more familiar and less fearful. We're only humans with animal spirits. I would recommend playing on a platform like EasyEquities and Wealthport to familiarise yourself with their product offerings. When you are ready, register your account and start investing.

7

Making your money work for you

By now you understand that you need to have the right attitude about money. You also know that financial goal-setting is of the utmost importance and that there is a difference between saving and investing. I have given you a few tips on how to budget and where to save money. You also know a bit about the stock market, the people who work in the finance industry and the different asset classes.

The options open to investors are vast, and you are not forced to choose only one type of investment. However, there are certain principles that we have already touched on that need to guide you in your investment decisions. For one, you need to take stock of where you are in life and what your needs are. If you are still young (in your twenties and thirties) you can expose yourself to higher-risk investments. If you are older than that, you need something less risky.

There are endless choices of investments for every individual taste, and I recommend you have a little of each type. You don't have to invest large sums of money in all of them. Plan ahead and build your portfolio according to your timeline and pocket.

First, everyone should have a retirement plan. Second, if you're an investor in South Africa, you should at least have some money stashed in a TFSA. If you already have a pension fund, you may want to consider topping it up with an RA. Remember that you can withdraw the money from an annuity at the age of 55 and there are tax benefits (see Chapter 1). However, you may not want to make such a medium- to long-term commitment, in which case you may simply want a TFSA. Whichever you choose, decide how much risk you want to take on. Start with the goal in mind.

If you are in your twenties or thirties and want to commit to a monthly investment towards your retirement, then start researching RAs. If your company already has a retirement fund and matches your contribution, then think about committing a greater portion of your salary into the company retirement fund. However, if they do not, then rather find an RA, which is a better option because of the flexibility and cost transparency.

Again, you get to decide whether you want to take on the risk and volatility of a pure equity fund, the stability of income or a fixed-income fund, or a combination of the two – whether the fund has high-equity or low-equity exposure.

If you are close to retirement, or aged 55, or think you will need the money within the next three years, invest in an interest-bearing, short-term or money market fund. If you think interest rates are going up (you need only read the newspaper or search the internet to find the opinions of analysts), then it is best to invest in variable-rate funds (money markets), whereas if you think interest rates are going down, then better to put your money in a fixed deposit at a bank.

Just remember that you will pay a penalty if you withdraw before maturity.

Unit trusts

You wouldn't believe how easy it is to invest in collective investment schemes, the most common version of which is unit trusts. I manage the Cartesian Money Market unit trust, and the mandate is clear – capital preservation and a high level of liquidity with returns that beat the bank deposit rate.

If you still have a fear of investing, try this: Google the Cartesian Money Market unit trust. Complete the application form, follow the instructions and send it with your FICA documents and proof of deposit to the address on the application form. And voilà, you're invested!

I specifically chose this fund because it is not volatile and you decide whether to leave your investment there for days or decades.

With unit trusts the options and combinations are almost overwhelming. In South Africa, there are over 1 500 unit trusts. To figure out where to start, you need to use yourself as the reference point to narrow down the choices. Start with your financial goals and position in mind. If you are investing for the longer term, and because you already know that shares outperform other asset classes over the long term, choose an equity (share) portfolio. You also know that the majority of your assets need to be where your liabilities are, so choose to be invested in the local stock exchange.

You also know that diversification is key to building a sound portfolio, so think about putting some of your investment offshore. Whether you want a generic global portfolio, emerging market exposure or developed market exposure is also something you need to be cognisant of. I'm inclined to think that if you are based in an emerging market such as South Africa, you would want to diversify into a class with lower correlation, and therefore you would choose a unit trust that gives you exposure to developed economies such as United States, Europe, Britain and/or Japan.

If your investment horizon is shorter, then consider being invested in yielding assets such as money market funds and/or bond funds. This process allows you to be invested in any currency or combination of asset classes you choose – it all depends on your risk appetite and investment time horizon.

From that simple exercise, we have already significantly narrowed down your choices. To further simplify things, it is worth visiting the website of the Association of Savings and Investment in South Africa (Asisa; www.asisa.org.za). They categorise the South African unit trust world into four geographic regions: South Africa, worldwide, global and regional.

If you are starting out, I generally advise that you invest the largest portion into the region where you are based, in this case South Africa. It is expensive to invest offshore, but it is a good diversification tool. When you feel you can take on a bit more risk, you should probably consider investing up to 25% into developed markets (US, UK, Europe).

Asisa further breaks down unit trusts by asset type: equity, multi-asset, real estate and interest bearing (see the Addendum at the end of this book). The only one we have not spoken about specifically is multi-asset, which, as the name suggests, is one fund incorporating the other asset classes.

The longer the planned term of your investment, the more equity exposure you should have in your portfolio. If it is a short-term investment, you would want to stick to money market unit trusts. Zero to three years is considered short term. Three to seven years is considered medium term and anything beyond that is considered long term.

At this stage of your investment career, general equities, balanced funds, income funds and money market funds are the most important ones to focus on. The pool of funds to choose from will still seem big, but there are some important guidelines and pitfalls to avoid when choosing a unit trust. Unit trust performance is only a Google search away. You'll probably be tempted to choose the best-performing fund, and whether it is being measured over one month, six months or a year, those periods are probably too short to gauge true performance. Remember that investing is a long-term game, markets move up and down, and managers' styles are not all favourable in all market conditions. Therefore, you will want to use longer-term performance numbers to get a sense of which funds have a proven track record. It is a near-impossibility for any one fund, even the ones that have been around for a long time, to stay at number one in the league tables.

One of the crazy sayings I left out of Chapter 6 was 'Past performance is no indication of future performance'. I left it out because it's not crazy. In fact, it is a FSCA requirement that when I show clients past performance, I have to warn them that I may not repeat that performance. Bear that in mind. Always. Do not base your decisions on returns alone. Every fund that has ever existed has bad or negative years, no matter how smart the fund manager is.

As nice as it is to say that your fund manager is the best-performing fund manager in the country, I would warn against any manager that sells you his fund based purely on performance. Believe me, as a fund manager, it's tempting to brag when your fund is rated best-performing fund. I know my clients love it, but that's when I get nervous, because I know that next month, or next year, I won't be the best-performing fund, and then what happens?

Consistency, a good reputation and giving the client what s/he needs are far more important than a fund manager's obsession with being the best performer. With the right level of diligence thrown into the above mix, you'll find that the fund manager is likely to hit the top spot fairly regularly over an extended period.

Right now, I feel like my compliance lady is looking over my shoulder and waving her finger at me. She wants me to tell you that past performance is no indication of future performance. Germa's voice is ringing in my head: 'Also tell them that Cartesian Capital is a licensed financial services provider, number 45318, and that this book is not considered advice, but merely an exercise to teach people about investing.'

The key feature of collective investment schemes is that they are generally tax-efficient and managed by professionals, and should not cost you an arm and a leg. Check the costs, do comparisons, and ensure you get what you're paying for.

On the subject of cost, I need to bring your attention to the discussion around passive versus active investments. It is generally accepted that passive funds – those that follow one of the many benchmarks established by the JSE indices committee (for example, financial sector, mining, etc) – are cheaper than actively managed funds. With actively managed funds the fund manager is trying to outperform the benchmark. However, history has shown that very few active managers beat their benchmark after costs.

What many people don't realise is that passive funds never beat their benchmark. If they do, chances are they took additional, unnecessary risk, which you did not factor in when building your portfolio. The reason passive funds should never beat, or even perfectly match, the benchmark is because there are trading fees, the market is dynamic, and you can never perfectly replicate the benchmark every minute of every day. And, of course, no matter how cheap, even passive funds charge a management fee.

All of these factors detract from performance. I see nothing wrong with a portfolio that has a combination of passive and active funds even in the same category.

Here are a few things to look out for in selecting a fund:

- What is the cost of the fund?
- Do you want to be paid out your returns every month or reinvest? In Chapter 8 I'll explain why my advice would nearly always be to reinvest your returns.
- Is there a minimum investment? There is an administration fee for small amounts; look for it and decide whether you want to invest a small amount or enough to make the fee negligible.

Particularly with money market funds, because we are guided by our benchmark and the interest rates in the country. As I write this, I believe we are in an interest rate hiking cycle, that is, the South African Reserve Bank, which sets the base interest rate, often known as the 'repo rate', has warned that we need to be aware that the US has moved into a period of rising interest rates, and this means that the SA Reserve Bank will raise interest rates should the need arise.

Higher interest rates are bad for those with debt, but they're good for savers and investors. If you have a floating-rate mortgage, or any other debt, and interest rates go up, it means your monthly repayments will increase. If you're a saver or investor, and interest rates go up, it means you should earn more every month on your rate-based investments, such as the money market investment you just made.

Pension funds

Pension funds are highly regulated structures that are managed by professional managers. You can start with the pension fund generally chosen for you by your employer. It will likely have the company name and will be managed by an asset manager (Cartesian, Coronation, Allan Gray, Discovery, Momentum, Sanlam, etc).

Historically, companies offered defined benefit pension funds, in which you and the company would make the requisite monthly contributions and your benefits were decided upfront. For the most part, companies offered you 80% of your final salary at retirement – and monthly contribution percentages were calculated upfront.

As you can imagine, sometimes the markets would not perform well, or you could get a huge jump in your salary at the end of your career and all your contributions would not meet the 80% payout ratio, or the pension fund had not taken enough risk and not achieved the required return to meet these obligations. This happened often, and companies found themselves in the position of being forced effectively to subsidise retirees.

Today, most companies offer defined contribution funds, which places the onus on the employee to ensure they have sufficient money at retirement. This is why most pension funds will offer you a choice of investment strategy. The most common strategies are growth (sometimes called 'aggressive'), moderate and conservative.

If you are young, you are likely to be put into the growth portfolio. This means that the manager will invest in more shares and fewer bonds. As you get older, the pension fund advisor will move you into the moderate investment fund, and as you get closer to retirement, you will be moved into the conservative strategy. These strategies are well-researched and have been used for many decades.

The biggest concern in the investment industry is that people are living longer. In the past, if you continued to contribute the maximum to your company pension fund and followed this strategy, you would be fine. The current maximum contribution to a pension fund, including an RA, is 27,5% of your taxable income. Today, unless you have not invested enough, or been aggressive enough in your investment strategy, you are almost forced to take on more risk at a later stage so that you can eventually reach your goals. In short, you are better advised to contribute as much as regulation will allow, and also to have a separate investment fund in order to ensure a happy (longer) retirement. As I mentioned in Chapter 1, the biggest mistake you can make is to withdraw your pension money when you change jobs.

Investing is very much like being an athlete. In your twenties you have time and energy to exercise, with less risk of injury. Training in your thirties and forties becomes more difficult. By the time you get to your fifties, running a sub-four-hour marathon is a near-impossibility, especially if you have never done it before.

I speak from personal experience. At 48, I am an erstwhile Ironman trying to make a comeback. Luckily for me, I've played sport all my life, even if I've had periods of non-activity. My 'comeback' has been hard, but not as hard as it would have been had I never played sport. In a couple of years, I will be glad that I made the effort to get back into it now, because the longer I leave it, the harder it will be – not to mention how hard it will be when I'm 70 years old and it's too late to regain sufficient strength and fitness to complete a triathlon.

It's exactly the same with financial fitness: start young and be consistent. Try not to falter, but if you do it's not the end of the world; try to get back on track as soon as possible.

You need to decide what your risk-taking capacity and long-term ambitions are. At my age, I am unlikely to be an elite triathlete, but I will risk cycling on the Johannesburg roads at 5 am to ensure I reach my final goal. I may have an accident or have my bike jacked, but my chances of reaching my goal are greatly improved by the risk I am willing to take. Sadly, time is not on my side, and if I do have an accident, my recovery time is longer.

If you start when you're young, you have a natural advantage. Make the most of it. Take as much time as you can to swim, run and cycle, and play as much cricket, tennis, rugby, volleyball as you can. Build a solid base. As you age, or perhaps pick up an injury, you may have to transition from high-impact parkour to low-impact swimming, but at least you'll have a high level of base fitness.

In financial terms, take as much money as you can to invest in higher-risk, higher-return products. Build a solid base by investing as much of your salary, inheritance or bonuses as you can. Markets may turn against you. You may get retrenched or decide that it's time to build your own business, but at least you'll have built a solid financial safety net. It's difficult to quantify a safety net. Only you can decide how much you need, but the sooner you start, the more money you will be able to accumulate. That safety net will secure your future, because as you age, you have less scope and it takes longer to recover.

Shares

Like making a Baked Alaska from scratch, choosing specific shares is a complicated task. For this reason, most people generally let the asset managers do it for them. It is our job to analyse the economy to decide whether it is better to be in shares or bonds, or retail shares or commodity shares, or whether the Foschini Group is a better pick over Mr Price or Woolworths.

If there's anyone who understands the excitement of analysing and buying individual shares, it is me. So, if you do want to build your own portfolio of shares, then go for it. It's an exciting prospect and intriguing to watch your shares go up and down (because they never stay the same) and to get to understand why share prices fluctuate. Do yourself a favour: read as much as you can.

If you're thinking of investing in shares directly, you know better than to buy only one share; don't forget to build a diversified portfolio, in which case buy high-growth as well as dividend-paying shares, and maybe even one or two speculative shares.

You need to understand where the world and your country are in the economic cycle. If the economy is booming and people are buying new clothes and cars, then you want to be in the clothing and car retailers. Again, drill down into each of the companies and see which ones are cheap, which ones are expensive, and which ones are market leaders and price makers. These are companies whose reputation ensures that consumers are willing to pay a premium for their goods. Does Woolworths come to mind?

There are many indicators, and it might be difficult for you to try and understand them all at this stage. However, I strongly recommend that you learn to understand a company's price-earnings (PE) ratio, because this is what indicates whether a share is cheap or expensive.

The PE ratio is simply the price of a share divided by the earnings the company generates per share. It's easy to find a company's PE ratio on the internet or the popular Bloomberg Business app (free download).

For example, if a company's share is trading at R100 and is generating R5 per share in earnings per year, then the PE ratio is 20 times. The multiple (times) basically describes how long it will take for the company to generate earnings per share of the money you invested. In this example, it will take the company 20 years to generate the R100 you invested in that company.

A share trading at R1 with a 35-times PE ratio may be more expensive than a share trading at R100 with a five-times PE ratio, so it's not about the absolute share price. However, it is not that simple, because a PE ratio needs to be compared to where the company has been trading historically, as well as to similar companies within the same sector and at the same growth stage. Not every company is at the same growth stage. Some companies can grow their annual earnings by double digits, while others are more mature and less agile, or operate in a sector that is staid or at the end of its lifespan.

Compare media giant Naspers, which trades at high double-digit price-earnings ratios (multiples) and seems expensive, to a company like Kodak, which trades at a multiple in the low single digits. One company has reinvented itself and is invested in modern, high-growth-potential businesses, while the other, despite being in business for 130 years, has not managed to reinvent itself for the modern age and is unlikely to grow its earnings without a dramatic shift in strategy.

Kodak may look cheap at a one-times PE multiple and Naspers expensive at a 50-times multiple, but, *pari passu*, your better bet would be Naspers, unless you're a deep-value investor who thinks that Kodak has a turnaround strategy that is yet to be understood by the market.

It seems crazy to think that an investor would wait 50 years for a company to be able to generate earnings that match the price the investor paid for it.

However, the stock market prices forward and for growth. If Naspers (stock code NPN) does suddenly grow its earnings by 25%, what will happen to the share price? At R3 000 per share, and a PE ratio of 50, you can easily see that the earnings per share are R60 (R3 000 divided by 50 equals R60). If NPN was to grow its earnings by 25% per annum to R75 per share in the first year, and the share price stayed the same, the PE ratio would be 40 (R3 000 divided by R75 equals 40 times).

Seen in comparison to Kodak, this still seems expensive, but in Naspers terms, it could prove to be cheap, as that company is able to grow earnings by a majestic 25%, while a company like Kodak will struggle to grow earnings by 25% per annum. Imagine if Naspers could grow earnings like that for five years: at R3 000 per share, the share gets 'cheaper' every year. Or, if investors were prepared to keep paying a 50-times PE ratio, the share would effectively increase as follows: at R75 per-share earnings and a 50-times PE ratio, the share price is R3 750. For year two, with another 25% growth in earnings to R93,75 per share and a 50-times multiple, the share price would be R4 687,50.

This is why it is important to compare the historic PE ratio with the current PE ratio, and also to consider the type of company, and where it is in the economic cycle, in order to decide whether the share is cheap or expensive.

Dividends

I've just used Kodak and Naspers to show you how to target share-price growth, but there's another interesting place to find returns, and that is in dividend-yielding shares. When a company makes a profit, it can decide to utilise that profit to pay off debt, to invest the money back into the business, to acquire another company, or to return the money to shareholders through a dividend.

If you deposit your money in the bank or buy a bond, you will receive interest. Similarly, if you invest your money in a cash-flush company, they will likely pay you a dividend and the share price will increase – sounds like a good deal, no?

Companies that pay dividends are generally profit-making companies. It's difficult to justify borrowing money and paying interest on that borrowed money just to pay a dividend to shareholders – even if paying a dividend to shareholders does buy a lot of loyalty from them. Nor is it good business sense to reward shareholders with a dividend when the company could make use of that cash to grow the business at a higher rate.

Therefore, it makes sense for more mature companies with stable profits to pay dividends, while high-growth firms and start-ups need to reinvest the cash to grow the business. It is also widely accepted that once a company decides on a dividend payout policy, they will stick with it unless they fall on hard times. Beware the company that cuts or withdraws its dividend.

When a company declares that it will pay a dividend, usually with the release of its quarterly, half-year or annual results (announcement date), the share is said to be 'cum dividend' (with dividend). If you own or buy the share while the company is cum dividend, you are eligible for the dividend as long as you hold the share until 'record date'.

Once the share is 'ex-dividend', investors who buy the share on or after this date will no longer be eligible to receive the dividend. So, what you'll see happening in the market is that when the dividend is declared (announcement date) or even leading up to announcement date, the share will rally by the amount of the dividend, or before the announcement, the amount the analysts and investors think the company is going to pay out. Once the share goes ex-dividend, expect the share to fall by approximately the amount of the dividend. Do not panic when you see the share price decline.

Be aware that most countries have dividend withholding tax (DWT), and that even if the company announces a notional amount for the dividend, the actual payout will be the amount less DWT percentage.

In a unit trust, dividends are generally collected or 'reinvested' in the fund. If you like the idea of receiving cash regularly, then have a look at the unit trust's distribution policy.

Capital growth

We've already spoken briefly about the increase in a share price, known as capital growth. But capital growth includes an increase in value of any asset, be it shares, bonds, property, unit trusts, REITs, etc. In the words of Warren Buffett: 'Price is what you pay, value is what you get.' My father used to say (it's bound to be a quote from someone else, but I heard it from him first): 'Something is only worth what someone else will pay for it.'

All assets increase and decrease in price, that is, they create or destroy value. Your aim is to be invested in assets that increase in value – in other words, that are worth more at the time of selling than when you bought them. Capital growth is generally measured over a time period.

If you're wondering which assets will increase in value, I'm afraid this is where risk and volatility are most pronounced. None of us know for certain what the future holds, and we are guided by history. For example, it is well known that during times of crisis, gold is considered a safe-haven investment, and therefore the price is likely to increase more than during times of normal or rising economic growth.

Think about this for a minute: let's say ten years ago you bought a piece of land and paid R1 million for it, and without doing anything to it, today it is valued at R1,3 million. Would it be a better investment than if you'd bought shares two years ago for the same notional cost of R1 million, but these were worth R1,15 million today? In very simple terms, your land asset has grown R300 000 over ten years, while your share investment has grown by only half that in a fifth of the time.

In considering the design of your investment portfolio, it is generally accepted that you need a combination of high capital growth and medium capital growth – because high-capital-growth shares tend to be volatile, and therefore score higher on the risk spectrum. The benefit of investing for capital growth rather than income is that tax is paid only on realisation of your profit. Say you buy some shares and in year one the market spikes and your portfolio grows from R1 million to R1,2 million. Unless you sell the portfolio, you do not pay tax on the growth in value. Then, in year two, the market declines and your portfolio is worth R1,15 million. Again, unless you dispose of the portfolio, you do not use the loss as a tax write down.

This is different to investing for income, where you are paid out monthly, quarterly or annually and have to pay tax on the payouts. I will never claim to be a tax expert, but it is worth looking into your tax status and understanding what sort of investor you are. Pensioners generally benefit from favourable tax terms.

You're an investor, not a speculator

For some of the reasons I've already mentioned, such as the tax benefits and the need to be invested long-term to maximise your returns, you are an investor and not a speculator. Speculators are looking for high returns, and are prepared to take the risk. As an investor with defined investment goals and timelines, volatility is not your friend.

However, for the speculator who is prepared to take the risk, higher volatility, shorter-term trading and scalping are what she lives for. A scalper wants the share to move quickly so that she can take advantage of the big moves. She is likely to buy a share in the morning and sell it on the same day or a day or two later. Often, trades are executed more on a hunch or some piece of company news flow than on pure fundamental analysis.

Every day the JSE's Stock Exchange News Services (SENS)[15] issues announcements in multiples of ten. Some exchange-listed companies and their subsidiaries can put out more than one SENS notice a day. With over 400 shares listed on the JSE, you need to be a full-time trader to ensure you don't miss anything. It is fascinating to watch a share react to a SENS announcement, but make no mistake: if you are not a professional trader, or you do not have one filtering the information and feeding it to you as soon as it is released, you stand little chance of beating the guys who do. We often call the news flow 'noise' – because often it is just that, distracting noise. So, unless you're a professional trader, focus on your long-term goals and forget the noise.

I've recently had the most interesting conversations with one of my cycling buddies. He points out that Warren Buffett, who is considered to be an iconic investor, is simply a statistical certainty; the fact that it happens to be a guy called Warren Buffett is mere coincidence. In other words, Warren Buffett is not special! Every investor stands a chance of becoming incredibly wealthy. If I'm in a pessimistic mood, I would say that if that is the case, then every investor also stands the chance of going broke.

Bear in mind that this book is aimed at making you a better investor for yourself, to reach your personal financial goals. If your financial goals are to make as much money as you can from the stock market, then this is not the book for you. There are a myriad of other books on how to analyse shares, 'read' the market, trade on technicals,[16] and 'get rich quick by trading forex'. Be. Very. Careful. Here.

Consider this book to be your entry-level investment knowledge. It sounds less exciting than becoming the next Warren Buffett or being an early investor in Bitcoin and then selling before the crash, but it's an undeniably important life skill. Of course, once you have the basics of investing covered and you decide you want to become the next Buffett, then I say go for it.

KEY POINTS

■ Start your investment journey by investing in your pension fund.

■ Start your discretionary investment portfolio as soon as possible.

■ Unit trusts are good building blocks for an investment portfolio, because they are professionally managed and tax-efficient.

■ Diversity is key, but remember to have the largest portion of your investments in the geographic region where your liabilities are.

■ Look carefully at the cost implications of investment products.

■ If you are younger, you can take on more risk, but know when to move to income-generating funds and assets.

8

The eighth wonder of the world – compound interest

To explain compound interest, let's first play a game. You will need two sheets of A4 paper and a box of Smarties. On the first sheet of paper, which we'll call 'Simple Interest', draw a line down the middle of the page and label the left-hand column 'Investments' and the right-hand column 'Return'. Then draw five horizontal lines at equal intervals to form 12 decent-size blocks. Number the rows from 1 to 6.

Do the same with the second sheet of paper, but call it 'Compound Interest'. When you're done, set this sheet aside for a few minutes.

Take a Smartie and invest it on the Simple Interest sheet, that is, place it in the first block (Investment column, row 1). Now pay yourself a return of one Smartie and place it in Return, row 1. Now withdraw both Smarties and eat your return.

Take your principal investment, or Smartie 1, and invest it in the second row (Investment column, row 2). Let's assume row 2 is year two. Pay yourself a return. Withdraw and eat your return.

Take your principle investment and reinvest it in the third row, pay yourself a return, eat it and repeat until you get to row 6. At the end of row 6, you will have one Smartie invested and one Smartie in return (unless you've already eaten your return, in which case you only have one Smartie).

Put your Simple Interest sheet aside, whether it has one or two Smarties; it really doesn't matter.

Now move on to the Compound Interest sheet. Invest one Smartie and pay yourself a one-Smartie return. Now, instead of withdrawing your Smartie and eating it, take both Smarties and invest them in row 2. Because you've invested two Smarties, you get to pay yourself two Smarties in return. So, there should be four Smarties on the Compound Interest sheet.

Move all four Smarties to the Investment column 3 (year three) and pay yourself three Smarties. Do. Not. Eat. The. Smarties.

Repeat the exercise until you get to the sixth row and have paid yourself 16 Smarties in the Return column.

On the Simple Interest sheet, you will have one or two Smarties. On the Compound Interest sheet, you will have 32 Smarties.

This is the magic of compound interest. Now you'll also understand why compound interest is known in investment circles as the eighth wonder of the world.

> **COMPOUND INTEREST** is interest paid on the initial invested amount, or principal investment, as well as interest on any interest earned on the principal.

The above is a fairly simple example, and you can easily convert it to real life. Consider the following: if you are earning a 10% return per year on your principal investment, you would double your money in 7,2 years. We call it the Rule of 72.

There's a very simple way to calculate how many years it will take to double your money if you know what your annual rate of return is. Just use the following formula:

X × Y = 72

where

X = rate of return

Y = number of years

If you are receiving 10% per annum, then:

10 x Y = 72

Y = 72 ÷ 10

Y = 7,2 years

Hence, to calculate what compounded return you need for a given number of years:

X = ?

Y = 5 years

X x 5 = 72

X = 72 ÷ 5

X = 14,4%

Note that the above calculations don't actually use the percentage in numeric terms. On a calculator, 10 would normally be 0,1; but in this case, we just plug in 10.

Furthermore, this is a simplified calculation because logarithmic values are impossible to do without a table or scientific calculator. If you want an accurate time period for doubling your money at a given rate of return, use a scientific calculator and the following formula:

$T = \ln(2) \,/\, \ln[1 + (r/100)] \approx 72/r$

where

ln = natural log value

r = rate of return

≈ indicates an approximate value

To find out exactly how long it would take to double an investment that returns 8% annually:

$T = \ln(2) \,/\, \ln(1 + (8/100)) = 9{,}006$ years, which is very close to the approximate value obtained by 72 ÷ 8 (rate of return) = 9 years

The Rule of 72 is reasonably accurate for interest rates that fall in the range of 6% and 10%. When dealing with rates outside this range, the rule can be adjusted by adding or subtracting 1 from 72 for every 3 points the interest rate diverges from the 8% threshold. For example, the rate of 11% annual compounding interest is 3 percentage points higher than 8%. Hence, adding 1 (for the 3 points higher than 8 percent) to 72 gives us the Rule of 73 for greater precision.[17]

Let's get a little technical, just for a short paragraph, because time periods do matter.

If you are getting a return annually (as in our above example), then the number of compounding periods is one. If you are getting a return semi-annually, then your compounding period is two. If you are getting a return every three months (quarterly) then your compounding period is four. And, you guessed it, if you are getting a return monthly, your compounding period is 12.

It's also important to know that while compound interest can work for you, it can also work against you. If you take a loan from a bank, for example, they generally quote an annual interest rate. However, more often than not it is compounded monthly (they don't charge you the full rate every month, they only charge you a twelfth of the annual rate), but they do charge you interest on the full outstanding amount the next month.

The same goes for investments. Banks are likely to quote you an annual rate, but take your interest compounded if you have the choice.

Watch out for the loan shark who charges 10% per month. Heaven forbid he should want to compound that weekly or even daily. Do not accept any such arrangement.

This next bit is for the clever clogs, because not even they want to build a spreadsheet calculating how much they can expect to earn (or pay) in 20 years at a set rate of return (interest) by putting in all the data for every year. And yet everyone should at least want to know what they are going to pay in total for a loan they take out.

In simple interest terms, for a loan of R100 000 at 10% per annum for 20 years (compounded annually), you would pay 20 times R10 000 in interest = R200 000.

To work out how much you would pay in compound interest terms, use the following formulation:

$$P\left[(1 + i)^n - 1\right]$$

where

P = principal

i = annual interest rate (in percentage terms)

n = number of compounding periods

In the above example, P = R100 000, i = 10% and n = 20. So,

= R100 000 $[(1 + 0,1)^{20} - 1]$ (0,1 is how we write 10%)

= R100 000 $[(1,1)^{20} - 1]$

= R100 000 [6,7275 − 1] (don't panic, even I need a calculator to work out $1,1^{20}$ = 6,7275 using the x^y function)

= R100 000 [5,7275]

= R572 750

That just makes me want to cry; I may never take out a 20-year home loan again.

However, if the reverse is true, then reinvesting every cent I make from my investments is a no-brainer.

We don't necessarily have lump sums to invest; normally, it's a small debit order per month into an investment account. I won't burden you with the formula, but if we used the above example and instead of paying off debt of R100 000 at a notional R1 000 per month over 20 years, we invested R1 000 per month at an interest rate of 10% per annum, compounding monthly, you could expect to have approximately R760 000 at the end of the period.

That is how we use compound interest in our favour.

Not everyone has thousands to invest at a time, or hundreds of thousands or millions to buy a home, but now that you understand the power of compound interest, I have listed a couple of tricks you can use to ensure compound interest works in your favour. This is apart from the obvious, which is to stay away from debt as much as you can. If you must take on debt, look carefully at whether it is being compounded monthly, quarterly or annually. Try to follow these strategies:

- If you can, make use of an access bond and pay extra money into it whenever you can. An access bond is great, because if you pay extra money into it, you minimise the interest charged but still have access to 'extra' capital if you need it.

- If you can, make two half-payments into your bond instead of one at the end of the month. Interest is accrued daily, and even paying a couple of weeks early minimises your interest charge.

- If you know you have a major expense coming up in the future (deposit on a home or car, wedding, school fees, etc), start putting away a little every month towards the lump sum you'll need. Every little bit of added interest and interest on interest works in your favour.

- When you're invested and you make a return, earn interest, or are due a dividend or other cash payout, do not withdraw it. Rather choose to reinvest the cash. In this way, your interest will be compounded on a higher amount, effectively earning interest on interest.

In short, if you must take on debt, pay it back as quickly as possible. If you are investing, start now and keep re-investing. Using our Rule of 72 again, you can easily calculate how much you will pay on a loan. If you borrow money at 10% interest, you will double the amount you owe in 7,2 years.

Amortisation

If you've got the general idea of compound interest, then it's easy to understand amortisation. In brief, amortisation means paying off a loan with regular payments as opposed to paying an interest-only loan and having a balloon payment at the end.

When you take out a loan and it is compounded monthly, the amount outstanding increases every month. For example, if you take out a loan to the initial value of R50 000 at an interest rate of 10%, at the end of month one your balance will be R50 416,67 (you were charged R416,67 interest for the month). If you do not pay anything towards the loan, your balance will increase to R50 836,81 (you were charged R420,14).

In month three, if you do not pay anything towards the loan, your interest charge will be R423,64 and your new balance will be R51 687,62, unless you are making monthly repayments, in which case as long as your repayments are larger than the interest, then the outstanding amount you owe will steadily decrease. Initially, the largest portion of your repayment will be the accrued interest and some of the payment goes towards paying off the capital.

In the above example, if you were paying R825 per month your monthly balance would look like this:

Initial loan	Month	Monthly interest	Monthly repayment	Month-end balance
R50 000	One	R416,67	R825	R49 591,67
	Two	R413,26	R825	R49 179,93
	Three	R406,39	R825	R48 764,76
	Four	R399,51	R825	R48 346,14

As you pay down the capital, the interest you are charged every month decreases, because the amount on which interest is charged becomes smaller. With the same monthly repayment, as the interest reduces, you get to pay down more of your capital, and that means less interest being charged. It follows logically that the more you pay on your loan initially, the less interest you'll pay. We also hate paying interest on interest, so try never to miss or be late on your repayments.

Let's take a look at another example to see what the impact will be on your finances.

When people take out loans, it is generally to buy an asset. This asset acts as collateral for the bank. If you do not repay your loan, they will repossess the asset (house, car, etc), sell it, and hopefully get their money back. The portion by which you pay down the loan capital is how much of the asset you effectively own.

Imagine that you took out a loan for R500 000 and only paid back the interest that was accruing every month. Your outstanding balance would remain R500 000 for as long as you're not contributing more than the monthly interest. However, if you pay back some of the capital amount every month, you're effectively paying down the capital and owning more of the asset. In the worst-case scenario, you have repaid half the capital and something happens so that you are unable to repay the balance. You could sell the asset, pay back the outstanding balance and still have the balance in your bank account. That's already the first benefit of amortising a loan.

If you have an interest-only repayment plan (non-amortising loan with a balloon payment at the end of the life of the loan), it's time to rethink your strategy. I get that it's easier to manage a non-amortising loan, because the monthly repayments are smaller and easily manageable, but you know better . . . no one wants to pay interest on interest.

For example, if you took out a R50 000 loan at 10% interest per annum, your interest payments would be only R416,67 (month one interest on the above example). However, at the end of seven years, which is what it would take to pay down the R50 000 amortised with R825 per month as per the above example, you would have paid R35 416 and still have the initial R50 000 to pay (R85 416 in total). If you had amortised the loan, you would have paid a total of R70 125 (saving yourself almost R15 000).

Heaven forbid you get into a negative amortisation situation, in which the amount you're paying doesn't even cover the interest. If anything should happen halfway through your loan period, you could end up owing more than the asset is worth, or having to sell more than the asset for which you took out the loan – not a good situation.

Let's take the same example as above, the R50 000 loan with 10% per annum interest, but with repayments of only R300. After year seven you would still have an outstanding balance of R64 645, despite having already paid R25 500 in monthly repayments of R300.

If you really want to be shocked, let's calculate the interest payment on your credit card, which is a non-amortising loan without a definitive end period. The first issue with credit cards is that interest rates are double – if not more than double – the interest rate on your home loan.

Say you borrow R50 000 on your credit card and the monthly repayment is only 10% of the outstanding balance:

Loan balance	Month	Monthly interest	Monthly repayment	Month-end balance
R50 000	One	R833,33	R5 083	R45 750,00
	Two	R762,50	R4 651	R41 429,17
	Three	R690,49	R4 212	R37 036,32
	Four	R617,27	R3 765	R28 029,76

Assuming you do not use your credit card after the initial splurge, in only the first four months you've already been charged almost R3 000 in interest and your monthly repayments start at R5 000 per month. If you don't pay down this debt as soon as possible, you will be continuously paying R5 000 per month and being charged over R800 per month.

KEY POINTS

1. Invest as soon as possible to take advantage of compound interest – you owe it to yourself.
2. Take out a loan only if you have to.
3. Make sure you know how interest is calculated and compounded (daily, monthly, quarterly or annually).
4. Avoid paying interest on interest as far as possible.
5. Do not pay excessive interest.
6. Pay down your debts as soon as you can.

9

Understanding risk

Remember when we invested in the Cartesian Money Market unit trust? I specifically chose the money market fund because it is considered low-risk and low-volatility. No matter how long ago you made the investment, it should reflect a positive return.

If we'd chosen to invest in an equity fund, there is a chance that the value of your investment today could be less than the amount you invested. However, there is also a chance that your investment in an equity fund could be worth a lot more today than the money market investment we made.

Volatility, risk, return, time . . . they're awkward bedfellows, but bedfellows nonetheless.

As they say of so many things in life, 'no pain, no gain'. And it's the truth. To get the reward, you need three things: 1) patience, which in investment terms translates into time (start early); 2) a good understanding that exceptional returns requires you to take some risk (pain!); and 3) discipline.

Ever hear of the Marshmallow Test? This was a simple psychology experiment done at Stanford University in the 1960s and 1970s. A child was offered one marshmallow and told that if she waited 15 minutes, she could have two marsh-mallows (sometimes they used cookies or pizza as the additional reward). During the 15 minutes, the child was left alone in the room.

The psychologist performing the test found that children who were able to delay gratification generally had better life outcomes, as measured by academic test scores, educational attainment, body mass index and similar measurements. Subsequently, there have been some questions around the diversity of the group and whether or not the experiment works across all cultures and under different situations, such as family and home environment and whether or not the child experienced broken promises around the time of the test.

In terms of the discipline it requires, investing is a bit like the Marshmallow Test. You can earn money today and buy yourself something nice or you can invest it and have two nice things in a couple of years. History has proven that the higher your return expectations, the more risk you need to take. That doesn't mean that you should be taking risks blindly, though. You should also understand that sometimes exceptional returns are not what you need, and that you require the preservation of capital and/or income.

In this chapter I want to focus on risk, because to be forewarned is to be forearmed. We've spoken about how risk can mean not having enough money at retirement, and also how a negative year for the markets can be a terrible risk if you need to withdraw your money. There is also the negative impact of not taking on enough risk when you are young.

In short, so far I've used risk in a very generic way. But there are lots of different, specific types of risk that can impact your investment portfolio.

Volatility risk

We've discussed volatility risk in quite a lot of detail already, especially in terms of the stock market. We've seen that volatility in the stock market usually generates higher returns over the long term. However, that is only one side of the story. The other is timing – not timing the market, but your personal timing.

There's no point in making huge returns for two years if those returns – and, heaven forbid, your capital – are wiped out a week before you need to withdraw your investment. In this instance, taking the risk of being invested in volatile assets is pretty much wasted. In reality, you could have been invested in safer assets that paid a yield and preserved your capital (read: possibly not made as high a return), but at least you have the money when you need it.

Here's the thing: you need to set a goal, but as you get closer to your goal (in terms of the return and your timeline), it is completely acceptable to move your investments into less volatile assets. A lot of people will never reach that stage, and unfortunately for them, they may have to take on the additional risk (in this case, volatility risk), to try and 'catch up'. That's okay, markets have proven that it's not a complete coin toss, and so most volatility risk can be negated by giving yourself time and having the discipline not to withdraw when the market is in a rut.

For many of us today, retiring at the standard retirement age is a real challenge if we want to maintain a decent lifestyle. And so our options are to work longer or take on more risk, neither of which are absolutes. Your company or your health may not allow you to work past retirement age.

The one thing you can control is how much risk you need to take on and how much money you withdraw. Your circumstances may dictate that you need to live more frugally than planned, not withdrawing your investments (or drawing down less) and staying invested in risky assets for longer than you planned in an effort to catch up.

I'd love to tell you that it's only for a year or two, but the stock market has a mind of its own, and it could be many years before you've 'caught up' to where you want to be. Some people never catch up, but what choice do they have? To avoid this situation, start early and ensure you have met your goals when you reach retirement.

Credit risk

Although more relevant to professional asset managers, it is still important for you to know about credit risk. You may have heard about countries getting downgraded to junk status or upgraded to investment grade and above. The same applies to all companies, including banks.

I suspect you've never thought about the credit risk you are taking with banks, but it does exist. And the only time you are likely to experience the full weight of credit risk is when a bank collapses, such as Northern Rock in the UK in 2007 and African Bank in South Africa in 2014.

You'll know that banks evaluate your credit score and whether or not they can lend money to you, and also how much. Not everyone earns the same or has the same ability or propensity to repay loans. This may come as a surprise to you, but the same rules apply to banks. Not all banks are created equal. Some have better credit scores than others.

Some have to pay higher interest on the money they borrow. Not all banks are able to repay the money they borrow from you. Granted, banks are highly regulated, and the Registrar of Banks will do the valuation on your behalf, but even that is not a fool-proof system. This is why the Northern Rocks and the African Banks of the world happen.

The bottom line is that when you are depositing your money with a bank, you are taking credit risk on the bank. You are giving the bank credit, with the assumption that when you need your money, they will be able to repay you.

The same applies when buying (investing) into a money market or other bond fund. What this means, practically, is that an institution, company or government with a higher credit rating – meaning they are more creditworthy – will pay a lower rate of return since they can borrow money more easily than an institution with a lower credit rating. Because governments have the ability to print money, they tend to have higher rating scores than the institutions that fall under their jurisdiction. And governments with more stable economies tend to have higher ratings than fragile economies. The same applies to companies, including banks.

I'm not at all suggesting you find out the credit score of every institution, government, bank or company you plan to invest in, but you do need to understand why some banks offer higher interest rates on their deposits, and why some companies pay a higher yield on their bonds. It's not a perfectly linear relationship, but it is a good guide, and so when you see a bank offering higher interest rates than all the other banks for the same period of your deposit, at least spare a moment to think why.

Interest rate risk

The talk of credit risk leads us directly to interest rate risk. This risk is directly related to the yield on bonds.

Remember our example of Apple Inc? They had a choice between issuing shares or borrowing money from investors. Borrowing money from investors meant they had to issue a bond. Investors bought their bonds (loaned them the money) and in return Apple agreed to pay the investor interest on the money they had borrowed. The longer the term to maturity of a bond, the higher the interest rate (assuming the same credit rating).

Because bonds trade in the secondary market, that is, they can be sold and bought during the life of the bond, the price of the bond changes according to how much time there is to maturity, so that it becomes comparable with other interest-rate-yielding instruments with the same time to maturity and as the benchmark interest rate changes.

Imagine that a company issued a ten-year bond when the prevailing Reserve Bank interest rate (repo rate) was 10%. A year later, the Reserve Bank decides to lower the repo rate to 9%. Suddenly, being able to earn 1% more on your bond becomes an appealing prospect. Demand and supply, and the fact that the market is fluid and transparent, means that the price at which the bond trades will increase, and thereby decrease the yield on the bond that was issued in a higher-repo-rate environment. The change in the price of where you can buy and sell your bond is called 'interest rate risk'.

Liquidity risk

Not all shares and bonds trade at the same volumes. Some shares hardly trade, especially if there are few shares in issue and the shares are tightly held by the owners or management of the company. Often, speculative shares or shares in small companies fall into this category.

The risk for us is that when we own these shares, but need to sell for whatever reason, there may not be enough buyers to complete our order. In this case, we may take longer to sell, or be required to sell for a lower price than we would like or than where the share last traded.

It seems an innocuous phenomenon, but this feature is particularly exaggerated in times of a market crash or market capitulation, when investors are desperate to get out because of the uncertainty surrounding the stock market.

Inflation risk

If inflation averages 5% over the next year, the amount of goods you can buy with the same amount of money in 12 months is 5% less. We may not have called it purchasing power in earlier chapters, but we spoke about how inflation diminishes purchasing power.

It makes logical sense that when you are investing, the minimum return you should work towards is above inflation. Where this risk is most prominent is when depositing your money in the bank or a money market fund.

We've already distinguished between investing and saving – saving takes place in the short term and is aimed at capital preservation, whereas investing takes place in the longer term and you need to take on additional risk to make a higher return. This is where your money market investment becomes very useful. The return you make will not be huge, but it should be liquid, relatively safe (note that even money market funds can lose money) and deliver a return above inflation.

Money market funds have floating rate returns (which means they differ every month), and there is a risk that some months may not meet your target of beating inflation. However, this risk can also work in your favour. If you deposit your money at a fixed rate, assuming on par with inflation, at, let's say 5% (inflation is 5% and your deposit is returning 5% per annum), if your fixed deposit is set for one year and inflation is calculated monthly, there is a risk that inflation will increase before you have a chance to reinvest your money at a higher rate (because your deposit is for a fixed period). In this instance, you will definitely underperform inflation. However, the nature of a money market fund allows the fund manager to keep pace or catch up with inflation because she can (and often does) trade on a daily basis.

Furthermore, if you find that the stock markets are too volatile and you want a bit more security, you can move money into your money market account without diminishing your purchasing power.

Concentration risk

Diversify. Diversify. Diversify. Do not put all your eggs in one basket. This is particularly good advice when it comes to investing. Diversification makes a lot of sense if you are trying to smooth out the volatility and returns of your portfolio. There is also the possibility that you could over-diversify, which is what happens when the potential loss you are trying to avoid is greater than the return you are making from your assets that are performing well.

Most asset classes and even assets in the same category perform differently under various market conditions. For instance, during times of economic stress, gold does very well. In boom times, commodities such as iron ore are in demand because there are more building and infrastructure projects and an increased demand for steel, bricks and cement.

Diversification helps to protect the investor from different economic situations. Imagine that you were invested only in iron ore and the government's infrastructure spending came to a grinding halt: your shares would plummet. Now imagine that you have gold shares in your portfolio. In these conditions, chances are that gold shares will increase in price and mitigate some of your losses from the iron-ore shares.

There's a fine balance between being diversified enough, and being over-diversified. Using the above example, 'diversified enough' means you hold enough gold shares in your portfolio to make up for the losses in the iron-ore shares.

Being over-diversified means you hold too little gold because you are also invested in other asset classes, such as oil, property, bonds, private equity, etc, and an upward move in the gold price cannot make up for the negative move in the iron-ore price.

In short, choose your asset classes carefully. Use diversification wisely, and do not try to own everything. Most investment professionals believe that a portfolio of 15 to 30 assets (shares or bonds) spread across asset types, sectors, industries and geographic locations is optimal.

If you are looking at building your portfolio using individual shares, bonds and property, it is important to do more work on this. If you are planning to build your portfolio of funds or unit trusts, most of this work is already being done for you, and your decision will be more about your appetite for risk and volatility, mapped against your current and future liabilities and cash flow requirements.

When you add an uncorrelated investment to your portfolio, that is, an investment that moves in the opposite direction to what you currently own, like the example of iron ore and gold (for now, let's work with bonds and shares), chances are that shares may be volatile but your bond investment less so. One of the possible scenarios is that shares could end the year 12% higher, while your bonds return only 6%, giving you an average of only 9% instead of 12% for that year. The flip side is that your shares could have ended 12% lower and bonds returned a positive 6%, reducing your overall loss from 12% to only 9%.

Your main goal when it comes to diversification is to have enough of the assets that suit your volatility tolerance level and will make the right return for you, and then some uncorrelated investments that will shelter you from systemic risk, which is the possible collapse of your main investment.

At the conservative extreme, if you are saving for a deposit on a house that you think you'll need in two years' time, then you will put most of your money into a money market fund. Given this span of time, there is little point in buying a share portfolio and risking the capital – you cannot time the market, and there is a chance that the value of your share portfolio will be lower than the initial capital you invested.

At the other extreme, there is no point in investing in a money market fund if you have another 40 years to retirement. You would not be able to generate a high enough return to meet your retirement requirements.

Time risk, aka horizon or longevity risk

This one is difficult to manage. You can plan your investments well and have the best possible prognosis to succeed in achieving your investment goals, but what happens if you need your money before you planned? Or when the market has declined? Or if you have more life than money when you retire?

When we build your investment portfolio, these are questions you need to consider and risks that you should try to mitigate. As we move on to building your portfolio, you should also bear these questions in mind:

- Will I achieve my investment goals?
- What level of risk am I comfortable with? Am I taking on enough risk, or am I taking on too much risk?
- What is the risk that I could lose money?
- What if . . .? There are so many unknown factors, but you cannot control what you cannot control.

KEY POINTS

1. It's time to get comfortable with risk.
2. Your biggest enemy is volatility risk, but it can easily be negated with time.
3. Inflation is a fact of life: aim to beat it by understanding interest rate risk.
4. It's a bit complicated, but diversity risk exists, so keep it in mind when building your portfolio.

10
Designing your portfolio

Finally, it's crunch time. So far, at a minimum, you've tested the waters with a company pension fund and an investment in the Cartesian Money Market unit trust, but these decisions were probably foisted on you. Now you can start making your own decisions and take your investment journey to the next level.

In this chapter, I will show you how to design your own investment portfolio. Sounds pretty higher-grade, doesn't it? But by now you should know it's within you grasp.

Some people want to be completely involved with their financial plan, while others prefer to outsource some or even all of it. Irrespective of how involved you want to be, there are certain things you absolutely must understand. There are things you need to know about yourself – your life plan, your goals, how much risk you are comfortable with and what types of return you're looking for. At this point in the book, you should already have a fair idea about all of these things.

Even if you are confident enough to manage your own share portfolio, I recommend that you work through all the steps in this chapter.

I'm going to assume you've compiled a budget, so you know what your monthly income and your monthly expenses are, and what you have left over at the end of the month. I'm also going to assume that you know your financial asset and liability position. If not, then complete the table below.

Assets		Liabilities	
Cash on hand		Credit and store card debt	
Property		Home loan (out-standing balance)	
Car (resale value)		Car loan (out-standing balance)	
Investments		Personal loans	
Total		Total	

The first step on your financial analysis journey is to establish **your** investment style. Below is the type of questionnaire a financial advisor will typically go through with you. This questionnaire will help you think through budgeting and risk-taking, and help you decide what type of investor you are and what your appetite is for risk. All of this adds up to your *investment style*.

I'm certainly not trying to take the place of your financial advisor, because their expertise is invaluable, but making informed investment decisions requires you to think through these matters beforehand. Besides, if you still decide to use an investment advisor, you'll be one of his or her smartest and best-informed clients, and that is the perfect situation.

Answer the following three questions as honestly as you

can, and then go on to the financial planning questionnaire that follows:

1   What amount do you want to invest?
    Monthly . . .
    Annually . . .
    Lump sum . . .

2   What is your investment term?
    0 to 3 years (short term)
    3 to 5 years (medium term)
    5 to 10+ years (long term)

3   Investment needs and goals
    Savings (e.g. emergency fund, deposit for a car or for a home)
    Education fund (if you have, or plan to have children)
    Capital preservation (to achieve real returns above inflation)
    Investments
       — Capital preservation (to achieve real returns above inflation)
       — Capital growth
    Pre-retirement plan
    Post-retirement plan
    Income generation
       — Capital preservation (to achieve real returns above inflation)

Financial Planning Questionnaire

	Questions	Circle the appropriate number
1	**What is your investment objective?**	Points
	To generate income	3
	To protect or guarantee invested capital	6
	Capital preservation (to achieve real returns ahead of inflation)	9
	To achieve maximum capital growth	13
2	**What is your investment term?**	
	Less than 1 year	3
	1 to 3 years	6
	3 to 5 years	9
	Longer than 5 years	13
3	**I understand the effects of inflation and prefer:**	
	To accept an appropriate level of risk as I require my investment to perform well ahead of inflation over time.	5
	To accept an appropriate level of risk as I require my investment to keep up with inflation over time.	3
	Capital preservation is important to me and I understand that this might mean that returns on my conservative investment are sometimes less than inflation.	1

4	How important is it to you that stable, consistent investment returns are achieved from this investment every year?	
	Not very important, provided that the long-term outcome produces an above-average return and outpaces inflation. I am prepared to accept some losses in the short term provided that handsome long-term gains marginalise these losses.	5
	I can accept marginal variances in the value of the portfolio on a year-on-year basis, but would not like this to persist for periods longer than a year. The overall return of the portfolio should, over time, outperform inflation.	3
	Very important, as I wish to avoid a position where returns generated from the portfolio are erratic and lead to volatile swings in my fund value on a year-on-year basis.	1
5	What is the maximum capital loss you would be willing to bear over the short term if equity markets fell by 30%?	
	Above 20% – I am prepared to accept above-average risk (I consider myself an aggressive risk investor).	7
	10 to 20% – I know that markets often fall over short periods (I consider myself a moderate risk-taker).	5
	0 to 10% – I can tolerate a drop in value, but not for long (I consider myself a cautious investor).	4
	I would prefer not to face the risk of a capital loss (I consider myself a very conservative investor).	3

6	Which one of the following statements best describes your first consideration when approaching this investment?	
	I am investing but I am more concerned about the possible capital growth achieved from this investment and its ability to outperform inflation over the investment term. Risk is of secondary importance.	5
	I am investing but am more concerned about the commitment to the investment term and discipline required in order for the strategy to be a success. Performance and risk attributes, while important, are of secondary importance.	3
	I am investing but I am more concerned with how much risk is being taken on in my portfolio and I need to understand the risks clearly even if this means more subdued returns. Returns are of secondary importance.	1
7	Which one of the following best describes your investment experience/knowledge?	
	I consider my investment knowledge to be above average; I invest in shares, make my own decisions on what to buy/sell and understand the risks of doing so.	5
	I consider my investment knowledge to be average at best; I invest in unit trusts, I am able to pick good asset managers and appropriate funds and I understand the risks of doing so.	3
	I consider my investment knowledge to be below average; I invest in bank products only (deposits and money market funds) and have very little exposure to other investment products or opportunities.	1

8	How do you respond to excessive market volatility and a large drop in investment markets?	
	I am able to adhere to a long-term strategy, comfortable with the fact that markets are often very volatile in the short term.	5
	I am tempted to sell after a year if things have not recovered.	3
	I will sell if the underperformance prevails for 3–6 months.	2
	I am very concerned and I am tempted to sell.	1
9	Which one of the following outcomes is most acceptable to you (bearing in mind that higher returns generally involve taking on higher investment risk) if you invested R100 000 for five years?	
	Best case: R250 000 Worst case: R80 000	10
	Best case: R175 000 Worst case: R90 000	5
	Best case: R125 000 Worst case: R100 000	1
10	How dependent are you on the proceeds of this investment and how much capital can you afford to lose at the end of the investment term?	
	Not at all dependent, I can take risks that may lead to capital losses at the end of the investment.	7
	Partially dependent, I would not like to be too risky but can tolerate a marginal loss of capital between 5% and 10%.	6
	Fairly dependent, this is a major component of my portfolio and I would not like to lose more than 15% of the invested capital.	5

	Totally dependent, as this investment should cover my future needs and I would not like to lose capital on maturity of the investment.	3
11	**You are (potentially) able to significantly enhance your return (above target return) accepting additional investment risk. What is your response to this proposal?**	
	I am prepared to take the chance and accept more risk than normal in pursuit of this objective.	5
	I am prepared to accept a higher level of risk but require a fair amount of certainty or probability that the return is really possible.	4
	I suppose I can accept slightly more risk in pursuit of a potentially higher return.	3
	I am not willing to take on more risk than I have to.	2
	Total	

Once you've tallied your score, see where you fit in the categories listed below, which describe different kinds of investors.

Score 20–45: Conservative/Cautious

You require stability and are more concerned about protecting your current capital than increasing the real value of the investment.

Score 46–65: Moderate

You require real growth on your investment. A fair degree of volatility and fluctuation in capital value is acceptable.

Score 66–80: Aggressive

You require higher levels of capital growth and generally have a longer investment horizon. Substantial year-on-year fluctuations in capital value and volatility are acceptable but in exchange for potentially higher long-term returns.

The financial planning exercise (which can also be called a risk-profiling tool) you have just done is a good combination of science and intuition. Many of the questions require you to provide a relative rather than an exact answer, and some of it requires your interpretation.

Without using the words 'historically', 'definitively' or 'statistically', I'm fairly confident that most people are more conservative than they think. Although not comprehensive, this risk-profiling tool is an important part of your investment process because investing is more about the appropriateness of the portfolio you will build than it is about your target return.

When defining target returns, I imagine that when asked, 'What return would you like to achieve?', every investor would say something close to 100%. Yes, we all want to double, triple or quadruple our money in the shortest space of time, but the reality, as you now know, is that investments will only deliver a return commensurate with the risk.

Building your portfolio is more about reaching your financial goals, understanding the risks involved, and managing them with a bit of fastidiousness.

Medium- and long-term investors will see that there is a distinction between a paper loss and a real loss. The volatility I have spoken about throughout the book generally refers to paper losses and gains. Some medium- and long-term investors look at their statements regularly and panic when they see a decrease in their portfolio. I understand that it is very emotive, but it should not be the case: as a medium- or long-term investor you still have time to make up the losses incurred. Remember, you will only realise a loss or a gain when you sell your portfolio, so don't panic unnecessarily.

The conservative investor

Goal: Capital preservation

Investment tool: Bank deposits and money market funds

For the conservative investor – the person who is likely to need the capital shortly or wants to preserve capital rather than making big returns – bank deposits and money market funds are the best option. When making a bank deposit, you can choose the term. Normally, the longer you fix your deposit period with the bank, the higher your return.

Money market funds are an amalgamation of instruments that mature over a period from one day to one year. The benefit of the money market fund is that you have exposure to longer-term investments, but with 24- to 48-hour liquidity; in other words, you can withdraw your money in two days without incurring a penalty.

Bear in mind that even when you are investing for capital preservation, that capital should at least keep pace with inflation to ensure you have the same purchasing power when you need to use the money. Statistics South Africa (StatsSA) measures inflation using the Consumer Price Index (CPI), a periodic sampling of the prices of a 'basket' of consumer goods and services. While consumer price inflation, as reflected in the CPI, is the inflation number generally used, it's also important to take your personal inflation into account when you are making investments.

But, first, let's look at consumer price inflation. In December 2018, StatsSA changed the CPI basket slightly, as they do every four years. The new basket consists of 412 products and services, whereas the previous basket contained 396 items.[18]

The idea of the CPI basket is to reflect South Africans' spending habits, and notable additions to the basket include convenience foods such as frozen pastry products (pizzas and pies), instant noodles, ready-mix flour and savoury biscuits and rusks. Sectional-title levies also made their debut, as did video games, car rental, car wash/valet, chicken giblets, beef offal, peanuts, pears, chewing gum, toasters, coffee mugs, toy cars and diesel. Just for interest's sake, StatsSA removed blank CDs, blank DVDs, pre-recorded DVDs and postage stamps. They also took out tennis balls, teapots, electric fans, automated pool cleaners, tinned sweet corn (cream style), tinned peas, spreads (such as Marmite and Bovril), ward and theatre fees in public hospitals, and board games.

You could adopt the StatsSA CPI basket, or you could work out your own personal inflation by simply keeping a tally of your monthly expenses and calculating by how much they increase or decrease every month. If you spend R10 000 and R1 000 of that goes to petrol every month, then the petrol has a 10% weight in your basket. If in a month your spending increases to R10 200, your personal inflation is 2% for that month – take care to keep that in check, because 2% per month is 24% per annum. Some people do not eat convenience foods (well done, you!), and some people do not take public transport, which is included in the CPI basket. So the best thing to do is to keep tabs on your personal inflation basket; it will also help enormously with budgeting.

To make your capital preservation investment more accurate, you could use your personal inflation number to manage your risk-reward strategy. Clearly, if your personal inflation number is higher than the national average, you are going to need to take on more risk; if it is lower, you can take on less risk. Always bear in mind that we want to minimise personal risk while meeting our financial goals.

The cautious investor

(Retirees, trust-fund beneficiaries, those who have earned or inherited large sums of money)

Goal: Income investing

Investment tool: Income fund

If you need to generate a regular cash flow from your investments, whether it is to pay bills, keep yourself fed, clothed and shod, spoil the kids or donate to your favourite charity, we define you as a cautious investor, and your goal will be income investing. Income investing is a close neighbour to capital preservation.

You basically need a lump sum of money that is invested in such a way that it will pay you a monthly stipend that will grow by at least the rate of inflation. Furthermore, the capital should not be depleted before you no longer need it. There's a little capital preservation in this kind of investment, with a fairly onerous cash flow requirement.

The investment product best suited to income investing is an income fund. This is the name given to a professionally managed fund consisting of yielding assets that can offer you a regular income depending on the fund rules (monthly, quarterly or annually). We know that high yields (returns) require a bit more risk, and we also know that capital preservation needs to be lower-risk. For this reason, the task of an income-generating fund is a particularly difficult one.

These funds are crucial in post-retirement scenarios when you live in a country that doesn't have a good social welfare or pension system. South Africa is not the only country in the world that falls into this category.

When the capital you invest is used to generate income and to continually fulfil your cash flow requirement without depleting your capital, a decent yield needs to be achieved through high-dividend and interest-paying stocks and bonds. But interest rates change, so the question is, how to secure high yields to cover the income you require?

The alternative, known as the 4% rule, is a generic rule of thumb derived from the work of financial planner William Bengen, who studied US data collected between 1926 and 1976. According to the 4% rule, at retirement you should withdraw only 4% of your capital per annum to ensure you do not run out of money (or, more accurately, to ensure that your money lasts for at least 30 years). By withdrawing only 4% of your capital, your post-retirement investments should be able to continually meet your monthly withdrawals.

If you are not concerned about how long the money will last (perhaps you're not a retiree, simply a cautious investor who wants a monthly income), you should be able to withdraw whatever you wish. Just be aware that the larger your monthly withdrawals, the less time your money will last if yields do not keep pace with withdrawals.

We've spoken before about how people are living longer, how medical expenses are climbing rapidly, and how you need to be in a debt-free position at retirement to ensure your money will last. Let's take a look at how the 4% rule works in practice.

If you retire with R5 million and withdraw 4% per annum adjusted for a 6% inflation, the calculation looks like this:

>Year 1: R5 million less R200 000 (R16 667 per month) = R4,8 million
>
>Year 2: R4,8 million less R212 000 = R4,88 million
>
>Year 3: R4,588 million less R224 720 = R4,363 million

In the above example, we have not included any returns you may receive from being invested. Let's redo the maths and see what happens if our investments can keep pace with inflation of 6%.

>Year 1: R5 million less R200 000 (R16 666,67 per month) plus R300 000 = R5,1 million
>
>Year 2: R5,1 million less R212 000 (R17 666,67 per month) plus R306 000 = R5,194 million
>
>Year 3: R5,194 million less R224 720 (R18 726,67 per month) plus R311 640 = R5,281 million

Of course, only you will know whether R16 667 per month is enough to maintain your expected standard of living. I propose we do the same sums for an income of R20 000 and R30 000 per month. At a withdrawal of R20 000 per month and a 6% return on your investments the figures look as follows:

Year 1: R5 million less R240 000 (R20 000 per month) plus R300 000 = R5,06 million

Year 2: R5,06 million less R254 400 (R21 200 per month) plus R303 600 = R5,109 million

Year 3: R5,109 million less R269 664 (R22 472 per month) plus R306 552 = R5,146 million

It looks as if your balance at the end of the year is continually increasing, but because your withdrawals are increasing every year, and your rate of return remains the same, your capital starts reducing in year 6.

Year 4: R5,146 million less 285 843 (R23 820 per month) plus R300 000 = R5,17 million

Year 5: R5,17 million less R302 994 (R25 249 per month) plus R310 140 = R5,176 million

Year 6: R5,176 million less R321 174 (R26 764 per month) plus R310 569 = R5,166 million

Year 7: R5,166 million less R340 444 (R28 370 per month) plus R309 933 = R5,135 million

Year 8: R5,135 million less R360 871 (R30 072 per month) plus R308 102 = R5,082 million

And so you will eventually run out of money in year 22. With a R30 000 per month withdrawal, increasing at 6% per annum but still only receiving a yield of 6% per annum:

Year 1: R5 million less R360 000 (R30 000 per month) plus R300 000 = R4,94 million

Year 2: R4,94 million less R381 600 (R31 800 per month) plus R296 000 = R4,855 million

Year 3: R4,855 million less R404 496 (R33 708 per month) plus R291 288 = R4,742 million

At this rate, you run out of money in year 15.

But back to how you can achieve a decent yield through high-dividend and interest-paying stocks and bonds, as well as real estate. In short, how you should invest if you're an income junkie.

It's easier than you think to find high-dividend-paying shares: simply Google 'JSE high-dividend-paying shares' or look at the list of shares in the newspaper. My Google search produced a site I regularly use – Sharenet. Dwaine van Vuuren, in a Sharenet article titled 'The JSE's Best Dividend Payers',[19] lists the top ten shares to own for capital growth and consistent dividend payments. He also explains that companies pay dividends twice a year (interim and final dividend), giving you the tools to compare apples with apples.

Another option when it comes to investing in dividend-paying stocks is to look at preference (pref) shares. Preference shares look like ordinary shares, but are paid a fixed-rate dividend and have a higher claim than ordinary shares on the assets (earnings or in the event of bankruptcy) of a company.

In effect, this means that the yield on preference shares is higher than the ordinary dividend yield, and often higher than the debt (bonds) on the company's balance sheet, because of the extra risk the shareholder takes over the bondholder.

To make life easy for the investor, there are a number of service providers (banks and stockbrokers) that offer a product that replicates the JSE Preference Share Index. You can choose to be invested in the individual preference shares or in the index itself. If you are going to invest in the individual shares, make sure you understand the liquidity and risk parameters.

Again, a simple Google search will reveal the service providers that offer ETFs; if you find the fact sheet that accompanies the ETF, you will see the top holdings in the fund. For example, the CoreShares November 2018 fact sheet revealed that their top holdings were: Standard Bank, FirstRand, Absa, Nedbank, Investec, PSG, Discovery, Invicta, Grindrod, Netcare, African Phoenix (the old African Bank), Sasfin and Capitec.

From here, it's not difficult to look up which of the preference shares offer the highest yield. In the example below, I have circled the yield columns.

Weekly Preference Share Round Up

Monday, 10 December 2018 — equities@absa.co.za | www.absastockbrokers.co.za

| Prime | 10.25 | Repo | 6.75 | Income Tax | 45.00 | R/E | 18.05 | BoE Rate | 0.75 |

Issuer	Code	% of Prime	Effective Prime (%)	Price (Cents)	Gross Yield (%)	Post 20% Div Tax Yield (%)	Pre Inc Tax Yield (%)	Credit Rating
ABSA	ABSP	70.00	95.8	70300	10.21	8.17	14.85	Baa1
Standard Bank	SBPP	77.00	96.1	8050	9.80	7.84	14.26	Baa1
FirstRand	FSRP	75.56	94.9	8000	9.68	7.74	14.08	Baa1
Nedbank	NBKP	83.33	96.5	898	9.61	7.61	13.83	Baa1
Investec	INLP	83.33	112.7	7825	11.20	8.96	16.29	Aa3
Investec	INPR	77.77	113.0	7100	11.23	8.98	16.33	Not rated
Investec	INPPR	95.00	104.85	9325	10.44	8.35	15.19	Ba1
Investec	INPP	BoE + 50bp	1.50	9600	2.73	2.18	3.97	Ba1
Capitec	CPIP	83.33	90.6	9500	8.99	7.19	13.08	Baa1
Sasfin	SFNP	82.50	116.8	7100	11.91	9.53	17.32	Baa2
Discovery	DSBP	100.00	118.0	851	12.04	9.63	17.51	Not rated

Issuer	Code	% of Prime	Effective Prime (%)	Price (Cents)	Gross Yield (%)	Post 20% Div Tax Yield (%)	Pre Inc Tax Yield (%)	Credit Rating
PSG	PGFP	83.33	118.2	7350	11.02	9.30	16.90	Not rated
Invicta	IVFP	102.00	127.8	8260	12.66	10.13	18.41	Not rated
Steinhoff	SHFF	82.50	189.0	4401	19.21	15.37	27.93	Caa1
Grindrod	GNDP	88.00	132.9	7200	12.53	10.02	18.22	Not rated
Netcare	NTCP	82.50	115.0	7400	11.43	9.14	16.62	Not rated
Imperial Holdings	IPLP	82.50	97.0	8545	9.80	7.92	14.39	A2

Source: absastockbrokers.co.za

Let's turn to bonds for a moment. Bond funds are used predominantly for income portfolios because of their perceived lower volatility and relatively consistent yield. Bond funds, also professionally managed, are invested in a variety of bonds and can also offer regular income with potential for capital growth. However, with the possibility of capital growth comes volatility in the value of the fund. Choose higher-rated bond funds such as government bonds for lower risk, and do not be tempted by the high-yielding bonds, as these come with . . . you guessed it, higher risk.

Real estate can include anything from real property to property funds. Professionally managed property funds are invested in a variety of property shares and can also offer regular income because of the rules around listed property shares (they have to pay out a stipulated high percentage of income). Property funds have significant potential for capital growth, but are considered riskier than both income and bond funds because they are directly invested in the shares of a company.

Real property, although also part of a growth fund, can offer a decent rental income, but be sure to do your homework when it comes to expenses, interest on any outstanding mortgage and stability of rental income. Listed property funds (REITs) can also offer decent yields but, like preference shares, are exposed to the share performance of the underlying companies.

A basic allocation of one third to each of the professionally managed income funds, bond funds or property funds could suffice to give you the returns you are looking for with potential capital growth, but only you know your specific requirements and how much risk you want to take.

Income, bond and property funds also come in the form of local and offshore. However, unless you have an in-depth knowledge of foreign exchange (forex) drivers and a keen sense of what the future holds, I would not recommend offshore allocations in your income fund. It will only mess with the stability of your level of income generation as the exchange rate fluctuates.

The aggressive investor

Goal: Investing for capital growth

Investment tool: Risky assets such as shares and high-yield bonds

If your risk profile showed that you're a long-term investor with an aggressive investing style, then you're likely to be a capital growth investor. If you're young, there is no reason you shouldn't have a large portion of your investments targeted at capital growth, because you have what everyone wants: time and the impact of compounding.

In the short term, the probability of having a 'bad' year in the equity market is higher than having a 'bad' year in the bond or cash market. However, as the time period of investment increases, the probability of lower returns in the stock market decreases, because equities have the higher probability of producing higher returns.

A high exposure to shares is recommended, but there are lots of ways to slice your allocation. Choose from the list of professionally managed equity unit trusts or benchmark ETFs available, both locally and offshore. If you're feeling brave, start building your personal share portfolio. It's a thrilling prospect and a great way to learn about companies, business and the economy.

If you're keen to buy individual shares rather than being invested in a professionally managed fund, you need to at least understand the basics. When we spoke about the long-only fund managers (elephants) in Chapter 6, we discussed the process that the fund manager starts with to decide which shares to buy.

If you open an account with a stockbroker, you can ask them to send you their research or take advantage of their knowledge and recommendations. The barrier to using a stockbroker is that they have fairly large minimum amounts (hundreds of thousands of rands).

If you're happy to try it on your own, a good place to start is on the EasyEquities platform, which offers not only cost-effective trading and the ability to buy portions of shares, but also some interesting research notes on individual shares. Moneyweb.co.za and sharenet.co.za are also good sources of information, as well as the free Bloomberg Business app.

How do you know if a share is cheap or expensive? Let's compare two retail shares: at the time of writing, Woolworths (share code: WHL) was trading at R22,00 per share and the Foschini Group (share code: TFG) was trading at close to R8,50 per share. Most people would hazard a guess that Woolworths is currently more expensive that the Foschini Group.

However, if you are to compare apples with apples, you need to know how much revenue/earnings/profit each of those companies is making. In analysing a company, we use the PE ratio – share price divided by earnings per share. (It's easy enough just to Google the PE ratio of a company.) In this case, WHL is trading on a 13,5-times PE multiple, where-as TFG is trading on a 15-times PE multiple. This means that TFG is in fact more expensive than WHL.

The other key indicator for most investors is the dividend yield, which simply refers to how much cash you will get paid for holding the share. WHL is currently on a 5% dividend yield, and TFG is on a 4,4% dividend yield. This information is also easy to Google. We'd obviously prefer a higher dividend percentage for our invested money. Although it is beyond the scope of this book, further research is required to understand what each of the companies does, what their historic ratios are, what their future plans are, and whether or not you believe in their management teams.

Investment products for all types of investors

Now that you have resolved what type of investor you are – cautious/conservative, moderate or aggressive – and you understand asset classes and risk, bear in mind that there are investment products run by professional fund managers that you can utilise. We've already touched on professionally managed funds such as unit trusts, ETFs and pension funds, which is the structure in which your investment fund is held. Within each of these products is a range of quite specific funds, including equity funds, bond funds, property funds and balanced funds. As we've seen, each of these comes with its own specific set of risks.

This leads us to the topic of real return expectations, which will equip you to decide which types of funds to put into your portfolio to ensure you meet your very specific return goals. First, a definition: real return is simply the return less inflation. For example, if your money market fund is returning 7% per annum and the inflation rate is 6%, your real return is 1%. In South Africa, historically, real returns for property and equities (shares) have been between 6% and 8%, and 1% to 2% for money market funds and bonds.

When we talk about target returns, forget the 100% return on your investment and consider how to build a portfolio based on the return assumptions with the appropriate level of risk. Knowing what each asset class can return will help you decide what blend of asset classes you want to be in.

If you are a short-term investor, you are unlikely to want to blend the portfolio as you do not want your capital to decrease. If you are a medium- to longer-term investor and need to calculate how much money you will need in future, and how to get there without taking on too much risk, you will need to know what returns to expect from each asset class.

The balanced fund

Deciding for yourself how much money you need in a share portfolio, and how much to put into a bond portfolio or property fund, or to take offshore, can be intimidating. There is an easy solution – balanced funds. These funds combine shares, bonds and property, and are divided into aggressive, moderate and conservative categories.

Balanced funds are also known as 'hybrid funds' because they are invested in a range of asset classes (equities, bonds, property). Balanced funds take the hassle out of deciding how much exposure an investor wants at any given time to the various asset classes. Balanced funds are categorised by high, medium or low equity depending on the amount of exposure the fund has to shares versus other asset classes.

Aggressive funds have a higher allocation to shares and can therefore tend to be more volatile, while at the same time expecting to make higher returns over the long term. Conservative funds tend to have less volatility, and returns are more stable but lower than the average aggressive fund. Moderate funds fall in between the two.

It goes without saying that if you are younger, and you are investing for the long term, then the aggressive funds are more suited to your portfolio, whereas depending on your risk appetite (a combination of time, volatility, stability of capital and returns), you would move up or down the spectrum from moderate to conservative.

As balanced funds combine shares, bonds, money market and property, it makes logical sense that these are not short-term investments. Aggressive funds are generally for longer-term investments, while the less aggressive funds are for medium- to long-term investments, depending on the allocation to shares.

Again, choose a fund that is suited to your needs, take care to compare costs, and note that these funds can be either active or passive. The ultimate choice remains yours, and there is no need to stick to only one solution. Choose a combination of active and passive investments across the asset classes.

Regulation 28 funds

In South Africa, there is something called Regulation 28 (Reg 28), which governs pension fund investments. In short, the regulatory bodies have agreed that they want to minimise risk and have given asset managers guidelines to work within for each category of funds (as shown in the Addendum).

Regulation 28 is supposed to protect investors from concentration risk (the risk of having all your eggs in one basket). For example, a money market fund cannot have an average weighted maturity of more than 90 days, and the longest maturity on any instrument cannot exceed one year.

The offshore limit for Regulation 28 pension funds is 30% and 10% for African instruments. This does not mean that 30% of the fund will be invested offshore and 10% in the rest of Africa, but rather that those are the prudential limits set by the regulator.

These rules were put in place in order to protect the pension fund investor by limiting the amount of risky assets a fund manager can have exposure to. Much debate has taken place around these limits. An example of one of the limits is that your pension fund can have a maximum 40% exposure to offshore assets. When you consider that South Africa makes up less than one per cent of the world's GDP, it seems asymmetrical that you are allowed only 40% exposure to offshore assets in your pension fund.

The flip side of that argument is that it is more prudent to have assets where your liabilities are. In this case, the assumption is that most South Africans will retire in South Africa, and if you want to externalise your investments or take out currency hedges, then there is opportunity to do so through other investment vehicles.

Multi-managed solutions

With the knowledge you now have, you can decide which type of fund best suits you. However, there are a multitude of money market funds, as well as a host of property funds. How do you decide?

A number of the unit trust funds available to investors can also be classed as multi-manager funds. This means that instead of your deciding which fund manager to be invested with, there is a fund manager who will decide for you which funds to be invested in. Rather than trying to decide on one fund manager, such as Cartesian, Coronation or Allan Gray, the multi-manager will blend the managers on your behalf.

In the multi-managed solution, the manager decides which and how much of the Cartesian funds to use, combined with the Coronation, Allan Gray, etc. Someone is doing that work for you, but be aware that they are likely to charge you for it, and you will pay the multi-managers' fees as well as the underlying manager's fees.

If you are comfortable doing it yourself, then it's nice to skip the additional expense line, but remember that that different managers perform differently under different economic conditions and market cycles, in particular through extreme conditions. You can also get access to a variety of hedge fund managers through a fund-of-funds platform such as Ashburton or Boutique Collective Investments.

Taking advantage of tax-efficient structures

Tax is a certainty. Do not underestimate the importance of tax-efficient investing. Some investors think that because they are not in the top income bracket, or are only 'small' investors, it's not important to be smart about tax structuring.

On 1 March 2015, the National Treasury introduced the TFSA. Initially, investors were allowed to invest up to R30 000 per annum into their tax-free savings account, and by 2019 that amount had increased to R33 000, with a lifetime initial capital limit of R500 000. (Note that this limit is initial capital invested, but the hope is that it will grow above R500 000 over time.)

TFSAs are specific structures that are offered by a number of platforms. When you open an account on the Wealthport or EasyEquities platform, which are only two examples of platforms that offer TFSAs, you simply need to inform them that you need a tax-free savings account. They will send you a list of funds to choose from and do the rest for you.

Key features of the TFSA that you need to be aware of:

- You cannot withdraw and reinvest later. Each investment counts towards your R500 000.
- You cannot skip a year and invest R66 000 the following year.
- You cannot change the allocation. If you invest the first R33 000 into a conservative portfolio, but then decide you'd prefer to take more risk for higher returns, you cannot switch from the conservative portfolio into an aggressive portfolio.
- You can spread your investment across different asset classes as defined by the TFSA rules.

You already have all the tools to make the investment decision, so choose wisely from the outset.

As we saw in Chapter 1, RAs have significant tax benefits, and therefore have to be weighed up against a TFSA. Unit trusts are considered to be relatively tax-efficient because there is no tax trigger when the fund manager buys or sells shares in the portfolio, but only when you, the individual investor, sell units of the fund. You avoid paying tax as long as you remain invested in your fund.

For those who reach their TFSA or RA limit, there are a number of products that may be better suited to their situation, but I cannot advise on these and recommend that you see a tax consultant.

The impact of age and administrative cost on your investments

The 20:80 principle stipulates that when you are in your twenties, 20% of your investments should be in low-risk funds or assets such as money market or balanced funds, while 80% should be in high-risk assets such as shares. As you move closer to retirement, this ratio reverses, leaving you with only 20% in shares and the balance in low-risk investments.

This seems simple enough. However, imagine you did not start investing in your twenties and realise you will not have enough for retirement. First, you would have to increase your contribution to your pension fund, and, second, you would be forced to take higher risk for greater returns, bearing in mind that you will have to tighten your belt and sit through the market volatility if it comes between you and a fully funded retirement.

One of the founders of Wealthport, Eugene Maree, recently shared with me a graph he created to show the impact of an extra 1% cost per annum on your portfolio.

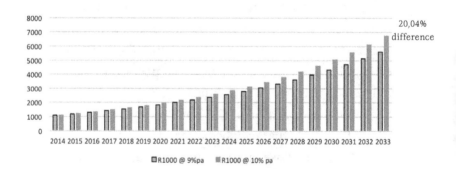

R1 000 invested with saving of 1% in fees over 20 years

Source: Wealthport

The graph shows that if you chose an asset manager who charges you a mere 1% per annum more than another manager and produces the same return, the difference over a 20-year period is over 20% – an amount not to be sniffed at.

KEY POINTS

■ Use the financial planning questionnaire to decide your risk profile and investment style (cautious/conservative, moderate or aggressive).

■ Understand the types of assets and investment products that fit your risk profile and investment style.

■ When designing your portfolio (choosing the assets or funds to be invested in), be aware of the impact of cost.

11
The rise of the robo-advisor

In the previous chapter, we went through a fairly rigorous, manual analysis of your financial position, goals, affordability and risk assessment. Now let me introduce you to the robo-advisor . . . you knew it was coming, because the future always arrives. A robo-advisor is simply an online tool that helps you decide where to invest your money.

Human financial advisors get paid a percentage of the products they sell. Because it takes time to build trust and get to know their clients' financial needs, financial advisors are selling their time, and we all have limited time. To make a decent living, they need to target clients who have large amounts of money to invest.

Enter the robo-advisor. The point of the robo-advisor is not necessarily to disintermediate the financial advisor, but to bring wealth management to the masses. However, the problem with every artificial intelligence system is that it's hard to replicate every human situation, decision, if/then analysis, opportunity, failure, motivation and outcome.

So, what the modern-day alchemists (IT elite) have done is to slice the analysis and investment process into chunks they can programme. Tell me your goal, and I'll tell you where to invest.

However, having read to this point, you know better. At least, you are aware that you have more than one goal. And if a goal-based online advisor is all you've got, you know enough to make it work.

How to distinguish automated financial advice from goal-based investing

Financial advice takes into consideration your entire financial position (including insurance and other financial decisions and situations). What many robo-advisors do is to ask you what your specific investment goal is (buying a house, getting married, retiring, etc) and then advise accordingly, based on the time horizon and amount of money available or required.

Ideally, you need to have already done your own financial analysis, and then reiterate the process for all your stated goals. After all, who better than you to do your own financial analysis? You can be as honest as you want with yourself, without being embarrassed about that little extravagance. You are completely in control – just don't lie to yourself; it serves no purpose.

Robo-advisors should also be cheap because the advice is automated and you are not taking up a human specialist's time. This is a win for investors.

Another great feature of robo-advisors is that mostly everything is on one platform. However, this same great feature is also a limitation. What most robo-advisor owners do is choose the underlying products for you. What you end up with are a number of investment vehicles and funds that have already been chosen for you, managed by the owner of the robo-advisor software. You become a captive client. The robo-advisor will sell only products that are associated with the owner of the software, and though the advice fee may be minimal or even free, look out for funds and portfolios that have high fees. While I'm a huge fan of the robo-advisor in general, that doesn't mean this advice is perfect.

Step-by step process

There are a number of robo-advisors ('robo') around right now. To take you through the process thoroughly, I have chosen the OUTvest robo – as you would have guessed by the name, it's the OUTsurance robo-advisor.

The Wealthport and Bizank advisors are available through the thinkbigstartsmall.co.za website.

As you can see from the graphics (from OUTvest) below, by the time you get onto the robo, you'll already need to have decided what your investment needs are:

GIVE IT A GO

What are you waiting for?
Let's get started.

Invest Monthly
I just want to invest each month

Target Amount
I have a target amount I want to reach

Lump Sum
I have a lump sum I want to invest

Tax Free Plan
I want to invest in a Tax Free Plan

Crowdvest
I want friends and family to help using Crowdvest

Calculate
Wedding, Education, Holiday and Emergency Fund Calculators

Once you choose one of the above options, you will need to know exactly what your goal is. Of course, by now you would already have completed the financial planning questionnaire and you'll have a good handle on where you're going.

All you need to do now is direct the robo-advisor. Give it the correct information and it will give you the correct solution – remember, with data and machines, the rule is 'junk in, junk out'. Your next step is to make a choice from another set of options:

What are you investing for?

Select a goal from the suggestions below and we'll create a personal investment plan just for you.

Wedding

Kick-start your marriage with an investment to cover those wedding costs.

Education

How much do you need to put away to put your children through school?

Holiday

Grow your funds to let that dream holiday take flight.

Emergency Fund

Invest in the safety of a fund that you can access in an emergency.

Just Invest

Put your money away to ensure you get the most out of every hard-earned Rand.

Start by giving your goal a name

And tell us what you are investing for?

LET'S GO

Throughout this process and with a few simple questions, the robo-advisor will recommend a fund it 'thinks' is appropriate for you. You do not have to choose this specific fund, but if you've been completely honest in your answers, then it's probably right for you. Based on a few basic questions around my income, budget and cash flow expectations, the OUTvest advisor spat out a recommendation for an emergency fund.

Even when the robo-advisor makes recommendations, note that you are allowed to make changes as you see fit, depending on whether you want to invest more or less, or change the term, and the robo-advisor will give you other fund options that are available on the platform. Although the robo recommended the money market fund, if I decide to change the fund, the robo will give me a couple of other options of CoreShares products it has available on the platform. Note that these products are all managed by the same team. By changing the fund, you are effectively changing the asset class you invest in and therefore your risk.

I hope by now that you have a fair understanding of risk and reward and goals and how you get there, but there is considerable risk that you might be more risk-averse than you need to be – most people are. Often, to reach your goals, you need to take on more risk than you would like to.

This is the big limitation of writing a book aimed at a broad readership. Only you can honestly judge whether you need to dial back the risk, learn to handle the volatility and take more risk, or be more realistic about your goals.

Robo-advisors are superb DIY tools. Utilise the advice and the calculators attached to the robo to help you decide how much you need to save every month to attain financial independence.

12

How to avoid fraud and investment scams

If, instead of explaining all the risks and reminding you in every chapter that making the right investment decisions was not going to be as easy as lemon-squeezy, I had simply said give me your money and I'll give you back 30% per annum, this might have been a shorter read. However, we have already established that investing requires a bit of understanding and a decent amount of patience. If anyone tells you otherwise, run for the hills, just run.

The goal of investing is to make money, and therefore most people are enticed by the offer of making quick, high returns versus a well-thought-out medium- to long-term plan. They will choose the easy money sooner than put in the effort needed to take the long road. This is why fraudsters exist, because lots of people want a get-rich-quick scheme.

Don't be the person to fall for the fraudster. I cannot cover all the schemes in a chapter, because there are so many, and new ones pop up every day, but I will highlight some of the obvious ones.

Pyramid schemes

Have you ever received one of those emails that ask you to forward it to three friends, with the promise of some form of reward or payback in the future? This is the basic premise of the pyramid scheme, which is one of the oldest scams around. Pyramid schemes generally do not offer sales of a product or investment, but rather rely on current members bringing new people into the scheme.

Let's say I put R100 into the scheme and find five people to each put in R100, I come out with R500 (net profit of R400 to me). Each of those five people finds five people and they each get R500, and then the 25 people each find five people, and it becomes a money merry-go-round, if you like.

To find five people seems a completely doable strategy, but the table below shows you how quickly you run out of new people to keep the scheme going:

Ground zero	1	
First level	5	Sure, you have 5 friends.
Level 2	25	And chances are those five friends have five friends.
Level 3	125	And in fact, even those 25 friends probably have five friends outside of the previous 31 people.
Level 4	625	It's likely that those 125 people each have five friends who have not already been involved.
Level 5	3 125	Now it gets difficult.
Level 6	15 625	

Level 7	78 125	
Level 8	390 625	
Level 9	1 953 125	
Level 10	9 765 625	
Level 11	48 828 125	90% of the population of South Africa, including children.
Level 12	244 140 625	
Level 13	1 220 703 125	All of China.
Level 14	6 103 515 625	Almost the entire population of Earth – note that it only took 14 iterations to reach this point.
Level 15	30 517 578 125	4,3 times the global population, including children.

The people who get in first make a nice little profit on their money, but pyramid schemes run out of runway very quickly, and the last people left holding the bag lose all their money.

Ponzi schemes

We've talked a lot about how best to generate returns, and I am sure the reason you've read this far is that you want to make some money. And that's fine. However, the vulnerable investor is the one who wants to do all of that without too much effort and as quickly as possible.

The name 'Ponzi scheme' comes from the Italian swindler Carlo Pietro Giovanni Guglielmo Tebaldo Ponzi (Charles Ponzi), who in the 1920s promised his US clients a 50% return in 45 days or 100% return in 90 days. When you're getting only 2% per annum from the bank and maybe 10% from the stock market, it seems almost ridiculous to pass up the opportunity to be invested for a 50% return.

Fortunately, you now understand the risk/reward continuum and where returns come from, so it's going to be a lot easier to spot fraudsters. For instance, you know that banks pay only 5% interest and that putting your money in the bank carries little risk. How is it possible, then, to generate an annual return of 10% without taking on more risk, or 30% without taking on exceptional risk, or even 50% without taking on ridiculous risk? It may seem obvious, but you'll be surprised how few people understand this basic concept.

I'm regularly found in the media commenting on the stock market and the economy, and in 2017 one of the listeners to my regular podcast, 'The Money Shot', on Cliffcentral.com, messaged me about the MMM fund. I hadn't heard of it before, but an internet search soon turned up reams of information about this Russian Ponzi scheme, which had spread to other countries, including South Africa and Nigeria. MMM is reported to be one of the biggest and longest-running Ponzi schemes to date.

MMM was started in 1994 by brothers Sergei and Vyacheslav Mavrodi, and Olga Melnikova. Initially they promised investors annual returns of 3 000%. Their marketing campaigns ran into the hundreds of millions of rubles. The scheme eventually faltered when Russian regulators cottoned on. Sergei Mavrodi was arrested in 2003, spent four years in prison, and was released in 2007.

Nine years later, in May 2016, *BusinessTech* reported that the 'Controversial "donation platform" and alleged Ponzi scheme, MMM South Africa has collapsed and rebooted amid what it calls a "media panic".[20] In July 2017 a *Fin24* article claimed: 'While online scheme MMM is growing through its rebooted pyramid in South Africa, the list of people who have fallen victim to the scam also seems to be on the rise', according to feedback from users. 'MMM froze its platform last year as users failed to feed the bottom of the pyramid with points collected from cash donations from members. A new MMM platform was launched in 2017, with a completely fresh pyramid to work from.'[21]

And in January 2018 it was reported that Mavro – the name of the MMM token/cryptocurrency –'will kick off on 21 January'.[22] In short, they went from traditional cash schemes to using cryptocurrency. This is not an indication that cryptocurrency in itself is a Ponzi scheme, but rather that it didn't take the perpetrators long to figure out that using cryptocurrency as a new marketing tool and an 'untraceable' means of exchanging money was going to be easy, particularly because of all the hype around cryptocurrencies at the time. I'm left speechless at the brazenness of it all.

One of South Africa's best-known Ponzi schemes was hatched by businessman Barry Tannenbaum, who in 2009 promised investors returns of 200%. Tannenbaum was the grandson of the founder of South African pharmaceutical company Adcock-Ingram, and used his lineage to convince investors, including top South African and British businesspeople, to invest in his scheme, which would invest over R12 billion in the chemicals used to make antiretroviral drugs.

The Tannenbaum Ponzi would have been difficult to spot even if the returns promised were not so extraordinary. While it seemed fairly feasible, it was all a lie. Tannenbaum fled to

Australia when his scheme was uncovered, and the authorities never began extradition proceedings. In 2015, *News24* reported that Tannenbaum was driving an Uber taxi in Brisbane.[23]

Another basic tenet of a Ponzi scheme is that the marketer of the scheme is a great salesperson and is able to convince anyone to be invested in some crazy ideas. Anyone remember the Kubus milk culture 'investment' scheme of the 1980s that left a sour taste in many South Africans' mouths? The originator of the scheme, Adriaan Nieuwoudt, persuaded thousands of South Africans to buy a dried plant from him for R500, which they would use to grow milk cultures. If they returned some of the dried milk culture to him, he would pay up to R100 per week, which meant that investors got their money back in five weeks. He then sold the 'new' milk cultures to more unsuspecting 'investors'. As you will remember from the pyramid scheme table above, he soon ran out of 'new investors'. Nieuwoudt collected R140 million before regulators declared the scheme illegal.

Not all Ponzi schemes are as obviously bizarre as the Kubus milk culture scheme, but it's best to stay vigilant.

Bernie Madoff

In December 2008, at the height of the global financial crisis, news broke of the arrest of Bernard Madoff, the chairman of Madoff Securities, an influential Wall Street investment company. Madoff, who was charged by the FBI with fraud, had been running the world's largest Ponzi scheme, bilking his investors – many of them wealthy figures in show business, high society and politics – of more than $64 billion. I love that Americans pronounce his surname 'Made-Off', as in he 'made off' with everyone's cash. Madoff's investors were lured by the unusually high returns he promised his clients – returns he appeared to deliver. As long as there were new investors coming into the scheme, the veneer of legitimacy was upheld.

Here is a simple example of how the Bernie Madoff scheme worked. He would take $100 from Investor 1, promising them a 50% return after one year. Then he would take $200 from Investor 2 with the same promise. After one year, he would pay Investor 1 $150, leaving him with $50. He would also take $500 from Investors 3 and 4 (let's say $250 each) and pay Investor 2 $300, leaving him with $250. And so it went on.

Of course, at the same time Madoff was paying himself a decent portion of the $250 he had accumulated. But after a while there were not enough wealthy suckers to keep funding the previous investors' withdrawals. And once a couple of people wanted to withdraw their money at the same time, there was suddenly not enough cash to cover the outflow of funds (because there were not enough new investors).

Inevitably, once a couple of investors don't get the returns they are promised (because of a lack of cash in the fund to pay them out), they need only tell a couple of their friends before the game is up. In Madoff's case, investors' recall of their cash amounted to $7 billion, when all he had in the fund was approximately $250 million. His take-home over the years was to the order of $20 billion.

How in the world could this happen? Bernie Madoff was not an unknown. He had previously held positions on the board of The National Association of Securities Dealers and advised the Securities and Exchange Commission (SEC) on securities trading, making him almost 'trustworthy'.

The only point to take from this is be vigilant. If something seems too good to be true, you should steer well clear.

How to avoid the fraudster

One of the reasons fraudsters fly under the radar is that they do not register with the regulatory boards and therefore are not monitored. The answer is simple: when you deal with anyone giving financial advice, do a simple search to see if they are registered with a regulator.

For example, Cartesian Capital, with myself as the Key Individual, is a Registered Financial Services Provider (FSP). A simple search on the FSCA website will show you the FSP's number, name, type, contact details, compliance officers and key individuals.

It is more difficult to spot the Bernie Madoffs of the world, who appear to be legitimate. Understand the limitations and risks of any investment you make. Always meet a fund manager in person, ask as many questions as you need in order to reach a level of comfort with him or her, use your common sense (if it's too good to be true . . .), and don't chase improbably high returns.

Unfortunately, sometimes even the fraudsters are registered with the regulatory bodies by 'renting' a licence. The FSCA is working on making Juristic Representatives redundant, but for now it is a legitimate scenario in which smaller companies who do not have their own compliance team, or the capital outlay to qualify for their own licence, can be registered on another company's licence. The idea is that the smaller company leverages the licensed company and compliance is covered by the licensed company's compliance team.

Where fraudsters rent a licence, the FSCA usually picks it up only when people have already lost money. The FSCA advises that you check that the individual you are speaking to has the correct licence, and if you do encounter a problem to report it immediately.

Another question everyone should be asking is this: is Bitcoin a Ponzi scheme? The short answer is, I don't think so, the reason being that it does not rely on new investors for the early adopters to get out. However, if you asked me if Bitcoin is a speculative investment, then I would not hesitate to say yes. To change my mind, you would have to tell me how you value a Bitcoin.

I understand that gold wasn't always a reserve for currency, and that at some stage gold derived its value from the demand by central banks, not just because it was a pretty and shiny metal, and using gold to purchase goods and services increased its value. If paper money was the practical solution, and gold is no longer used as a reserve, then how does gold still derive intrinsic value apart from its uses for jewellery? Furthermore, if cryptocurrencies are to replace traditional forms of money, does that make gold, paper money, coins and banks obsolete?

Absolutely.

However, currencies derive their value from something besides simple demand. The value of a country's currency is derived from investor demand and government supply, and some clever traders will tell you that value also stems from economic indicators, such as current account balances, debt level, production, interest rates, inflation rates and political stability.

I believe that the true value of cryptocurrency lies in the blockchain, and that there is a use for cryptocurrency besides its original use on the dark web. Which of the many cryptocurrencies will emerge as the 'winner'? This is a question for the future. If you decide to buy Bitcoin, you are hoping that the demand will outstrip the supply, or that it will be the one quintessential cryptocurrency for the future. It may not be the definition of a pyramid or Ponzi scheme, but sounds a lot like speculation to me.

We're here to make money – to take your hard-earned cash and invest it in products that will give you positive returns. Bearing this in mind, it is apparent that every investor is potentially a target of a pyramid or Ponzi scheme. Apart from checking the credentials of your financial advisor and fund manager through the FSCA, the best advice I can offer is to stay vigilant. It's your money, you've worked very hard for it, and you need to protect it as much as you need to make it work for you.

13
Putting the whole picture together

Investing your hard-earned cash is a methodical process that requires insights and patience. These are your basic steps to creating financial independence:

Starting point
Start by understanding your personal financial goals and appetite for risk.

Budgeting
In order to reach your financial goals, it is a prerequisite that you don't spend more than you earn, and that you save and invest a decent amount of your earnings. In this regard, budgeting is the most important tool you can use.

Get rid of unnecessary debt
Not everyone can pay cash for their home, but you should not be buying consumables on credit. Don't be tempted to be a fashion pony if you cannot pay cash for it.

Saving versus investing

Short-term goals can be classified as saving because you are putting away money in order for it to grow, at minimum in line with inflation, while not wanting to risk your initial capital. Your best options are bank deposits or money market accounts. Other investments require you to take volatility risk. Because you will want to withdraw in the near term, you want to ensure that your capital amount never decreases below your initial investment.

Timeframe

Start investing as soon as you can. Even if you are not sure yet, just put money into a conservative product and keep adding to it. You can change your mind at a later stage when you are more familiar with investment products.

Goal-setting

Before you start investing, outline your medium- and long-term goals. Don't simply know that you need to retire; think about how much money you will need at retirement. How much of a monthly income do you need to live off? Will your debts be paid off? For non-retirement financial goals, realise that every unnecessary purchase detracts from reaching your goals.

Build a diversified portfolio

You will want to start with a diversified portfolio that gives you exposure across a range of regions and asset classes.

Be realistic

Know that attempting to double your money in two or three years is an unlikely scenario.

Pay attention to cost

When choosing the funds to be invested in, or the platform on which you are going to trade shares, take a couple of hours to do a cost comparison. It'll save you much heartache and a good amount of money down the line.

Invest more

Continually add to your investments. Do not withdraw your pension fund if you change jobs, and always add to your discretionary investments.

Most importantly, enjoy the journey of making your money work for you.

Addendum

The fund classification used by the Association of Savings and Investment in South Africa (Asisa).

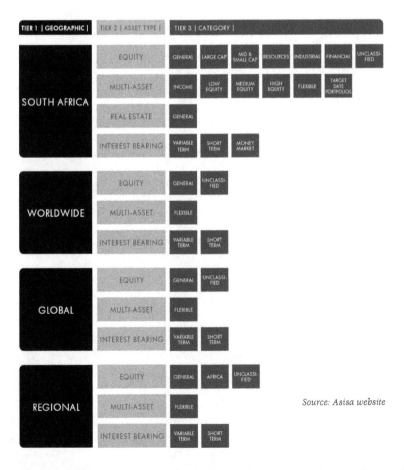

Source: Asisa website

Acknowledgements

This book was written for every person who has ever wondered about the seemingly fantastical world of stock markets and investing.

Some people have played more direct roles than others. First of all, my thanks go to my sister, Leila, and brother-in-law, Lester, who trust me with their savings and were worried they didn't know enough, but knew enough to get professional help.

To my family, Errol, Mer, Neil and Joy, your support is immeasurable.

Thanks to my friends: Mary-Anne, for reminding me to laugh at myself when book writing gets serious; Madeleine and her tall family, for your unending words of support; Judith, for inspiration and guidance; Sue, for the 'You know you can, now get on and do it'; Adriano, for the discussions on budgeting and Mark, for information on RAs.

Even if he didn't know about the book until the end, thanks to Glen for starting me in the world of finance and for your ongoing support.

So Yum and Dolci Café, thanks for keeping me fed and watered when my home became too claustrophobic during the writing process.

Thanks to the whole team at Jonathan Ball Publishers: Ester, what a great idea; Annie, you made it fun while being a huge help – everyone should be so lucky to meet a publisher like you; and Alfred, how wonderful to have such a careful editor go through the book.

Finally, my thanks to the people I am happy to lose sleep over – my clients.